STEP·BY·STEP

TENNIS

WITHDRAWN

Sue Rich

GALLERY BOOKS

EAU CLAIRE DISTRICT LIBRARY

An Imprint of W.H. Smith Publishers Inc

112 Madison Avenue
New York City 10016

© **The Automobile Association, 1990**
Fanum House,
Basing View,
Basingstoke RG21 2EA
United Kingdom

ISBN: 0-8317-8051-7

This edition published in 1991 by Gallery Books, an
imprint of W.H. Smith Publishers, Inc., 112 Madison
Avenue, New York, New York 10016

Gallery Books are available for bulk purchase for
sales promotions and premium use. For details write
or telephone the Manager of Special Sales, W.H.
Smith Publishers, Inc., 112 Madison Avenue, New
York, New York 10016. (212) 532-6600

The contents of this book are believed correct at the
time of printing. Nevertheless, the Publishers cannot
accept any responsibility for any errors or omissions
in the details given.

CREDITS

Author: Sue Rich
Photography: Michael Cole Camerawork
Illustrations: Oxford Illustrators Ltd.

Typesetting by Microset Graphics Ltd., Basingstoke,
United Kingdom
Color separation by Fotographics Ltd., London and
Hong Kong
Printed and bound by L.E.G.O. SpA, Italy

Cover: Gabriella Sabatini in action (Sporting Pictures
(UK) Ltd.)
Title page: Gabriella Sabatini playing at Wimbledon
(Allsport Photographic)

CONTENTS

FOREWORD 4-5

INTRODUCTION 6-7

EQUIPMENT AND CLOTHING 8-9

BASIC GRIPS 10-15

THE FOREHAND DRIVE 16-17

THE BACKHAND DRIVE 18-21

THE SERVICE 22-25

THE RETURN OF SERVE 26-27

THE FOREHAND VOLLEY 28-29

THE BACKHAND VOLLEY 30-31

VOLLEY VARIATIONS 32-35

THE SMASH 36-37

THE LOB 38-39

THE DROP SHOT 40-41

USE OF SPIN ON THE GROUND STROKES ... 42-43

USE OF TOPSPIN ON THE BACKHAND 44-45

THE SLICE BACKHAND 46-47

USE OF SPIN ON THE SERVE 48-51

DOUBLES 52-53

ACTION STUDIES 54-59

MENTAL APPROACH 60-61

SCORING 62-63

FITNESS AND TRAINING 64-67

TESTING YOURSELF 68-69

GLOSSARY 70-72

INDEX 73

FOREWORD

Tennis is one of the most fascinating sports you will ever play. It is also a game for players of all ages. Not only can it be highly competitive and rewarding, but also very social. It is a good form of exercise. It can be played indoors or outdoors, winter and summer, by men and women (although for the purposes of this book the player is referred to as "he"), and requires a minimum of one other person.

The very nature of the game requires hand-eye coordination and some racket and ball skills, but once you can hit the ball over the net you can have a lot of fun. Tennis does have a high skill level, and if you want to reach the top, it is imperative that you work on the skills of the game. One way to do this is by looking at top players and watching how they play shots, the tactics they use, their emotions and the way they react to success and failure. There is no greater feeling of satisfaction than when you've hit a good shot or finally mastered the backhand and have hit the ball over the net. The more you experience this feeling, the more you will enjoy the game. So read on and try to learn from the stars.

Each technique in this book has a difficulty rating, denoted by one, two or three tennis player symbols. One player indicates that the skill is relatively easy to learn, whereas three players indicate that the skill is much harder.

Also included are STAR TIPS, which might help you to master the shots more easily.

I have been involved in tennis for many years, and have spent the last 10 of them developing and coaching tennis — mainly with players aged between six and 18 years. During this time I have traveled to many tennis-playing countries and have experienced both the successes and the failures of my pupils. I have coached young players from grass-roots to international level, and gain most pleasure from helping people to fulfil their potential. One day I hope this will even mean producing a Wimbledon or U.S. Open Champion — perhaps it could be you. I hope you will get as much pleasure from reading this book and playing tennis as I do.

THIRD TIME LUCKY
Swedish player Stefan Edberg holds aloft the Wimbledon Men's Singles Trophy, after beating West German defender Boris Becker in 1990. This was the third successive Wimbledon final in which Edberg had met Becker. (Picture: Allsport Photographic/Bob Martin)

S.E. Rich.

Sue Rich

INTRODUCTION

Tennis is a complex game for two players (singles) or four players (doubles). It is a sport that can be played at any age from four to 80 years, although it is recommended that young children initially try short tennis — a scaled-down version of the big game. It is a sport for life, a wonderful and most enjoyable form of exercise for people of all ages and abilities.

The aim of the game is simply to hit the ball over the net and into a rectangle one more time than your opponent. It sounds simple, but your opponent is trying to hit the ball away from you and force you to run and retrieve the ball to make the game as difficult as possible for you. One of the great advantages of tennis is that it is a very adaptable game. It is also an excellent game to play just for fun. However, it can also be very demanding, testing the fitness, skill and competitive spirit of its players.

Tennis originated as an outdoor version of the game called Real Tennis. Although nobody in particular can claim to have invented the game, an Englishman by the name of Major Clopton Wingfield patented a game in the early 1870s which he called "sphairistike" and which later came to be known as Lawn Tennis. The game was played initially by the leisured classes, usually as a garden-party activity. Its popularity soon spread, and today Lawn Tennis is played in most countries of the world. The influence of the media, and of television in particular, with its live coverage of matches, has greatly encouraged the popularity of tennis. This, together with the advent of new technology (which has helped to transform both tennis rackets and tennis court surfaces) and the increasing availability of indoor facilities now means that tennis is a sport that can be played at any time of the day or year.

THE COURT

Generally a tennis court has both singles and doubles markings, as shown in the diagram. When a combined singles and doubles court is used, with a doubles net for a singles match, then the net should be supported by "singles sticks" to a height of 3 ft 6 in (1.07m). The singles sticks are positioned 3 ft (0.91m) outside the singles court on each side. In both cases, the net should be 3 ft (0.91m) high at the center.

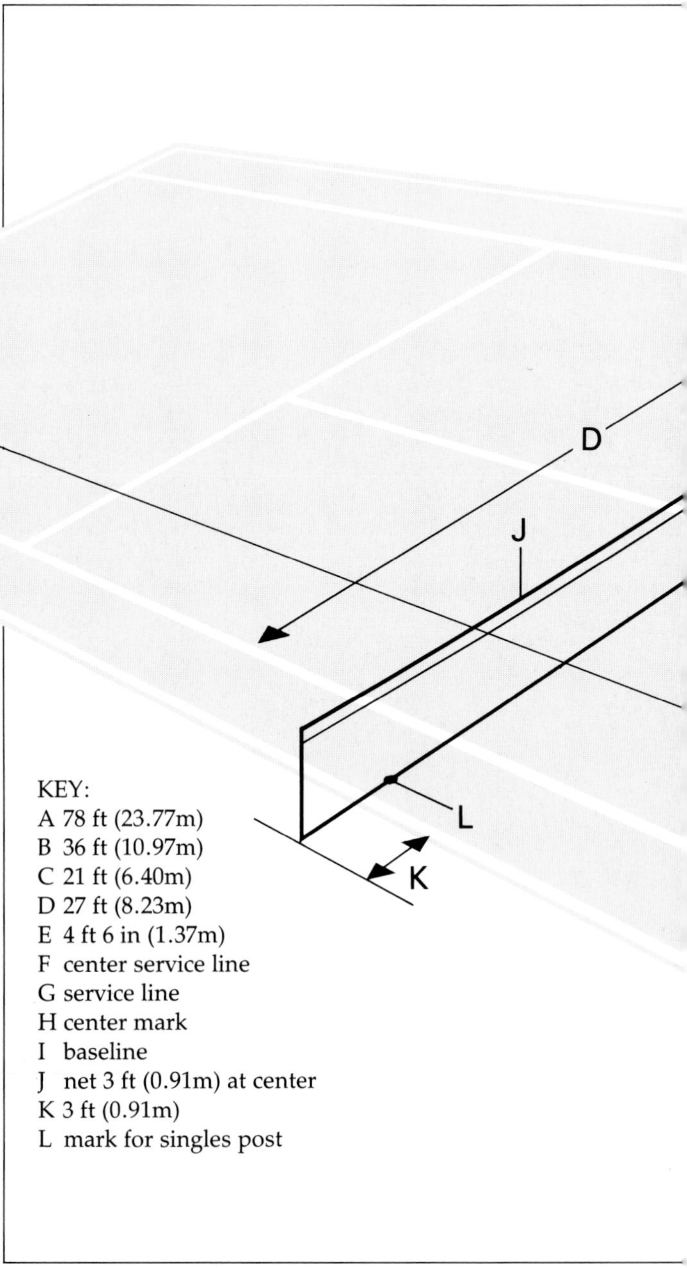

KEY:
A 78 ft (23.77m)
B 36 ft (10.97m)
C 21 ft (6.40m)
D 27 ft (8.23m)
E 4 ft 6 in (1.37m)
F center service line
G service line
H center mark
I baseline
J net 3 ft (0.91m) at center
K 3 ft (0.91m)
L mark for singles post

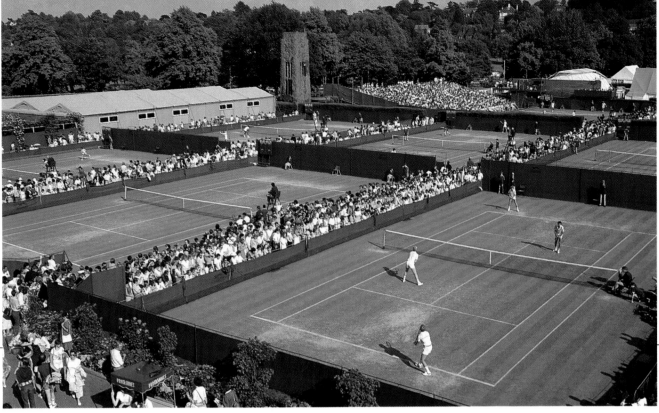

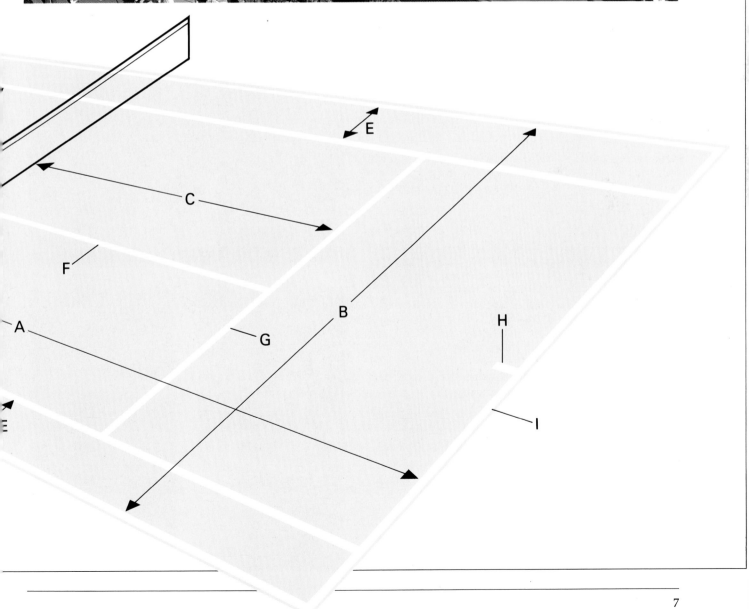

EQUIPMENT AND CLOTHING

To play tennis, all you need is a pair of tennis shoes, some comfortable clothing, a racket and balls, and, naturally, a court and some opposition.

It all sounds very simple, but there is such a variety of equipment available today that you should take care before buying expensive items. When you start to play tennis you may be faced with players who have expensive equipment. The cost of an item, however, is not important. The racket, and other equipment, that *is* right for you is the one that *feels* right for you. The most important piece of equipment is your tennis racket. If at all possible, seek the advice of a tennis professional or expert before purchasing your racket. There is a wide range of rackets on the market for all ages and standards of players. It is vital that you choose a racket which suits you, even if it means spending a little more money. There are several junior rackets available for five- to 10-year-olds, in addition to the small plastic rackets, which are especially popular in Europe for playing short tennis.

COLORS
Here you see Gabriela Sabatini dressed in white. As you will see from the photographs in this book, many colors are available. White, however, is still very popular, and is the rule in some tournaments.

GRIP SIZE
As a general rule, a player with a large hand will need a larger grip size than a player with a small hand. The grips on a full-size racket range from size 1 (with a circumference of 4$\frac{1}{8}$ in − 10.5cm) to size 5 (4$\frac{5}{8}$ in − 11.7cm). Recently there has been a trend for players to use smaller grips, but be careful because small grips can lead to elbow injury problems. As a rough guideline, when you grip the racket firmly your thumb and forefinger should just be able to touch each other around the grip.

The player is seen adding an extra grip to his racket to help him to hold the racket firmly while playing.

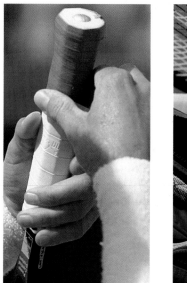

WEIGHT
The weight of a racket can range from 11 oz (300g) to 13 oz (377g). Modern graphite rackets are generally light. They range from ESL (extra super light), to SL (super light), to L (light), to LM (light medium) and M (medium). A young, small player would be more suited to a super light or light rather than a medium racket.

If a junior has a racket that is too heavy, it tends to drag the wrist down. This often makes it difficult to develop good techniques at an early age.

STRINGING

The two main types of string are gut (natural) and nylon (synthetic). Gut is far more expensive than nylon, but is more elastic and yields more to the ball. Synthetic strings are cheaper and can be used in any weather conditions. Many of the professional players use gut. The tension of the strings in their rackets will depend largely on their own style of play and, perhaps, the court surface on which they are playing. The tension of the strings in your racket will depend partly on the manufacturer's recommendations and your own individual style of play. Top players will have several rackets at the same tension, in case strings break during a match.

TENNIS BALLS

There are many types of tennis ball – and a range of colors. The most popular color is yellow, which is now used at Wimbledon (after numerous years of the traditional white ball). Some tennis balls are also now specifically designed for hard-wearing surfaces.

New tennis balls are expensive. If you are just starting the game, don't worry about spending a fortune on tennis balls. Get hold of some older ones and see if you like the game first. The better your standard of play, the more essential it is for you to use good-quality tennis balls. Once the ball loses its cover and becomes bare, it tends to fly through the air and is very difficult to control. On the professional circuit, tennis balls are changed several times during the course of a match.

CLOTHING

Although traditional tennis attire is white, and many clubs and some tournaments continue to adhere to this, a wide range of colors is available today. Always use clothing that is comfortable and allows plenty of room for movement. Absorbent material is useful, as you may find you sweat freely when playing tennis. Sweatbands on the wrist and head help to mop up perspiration and, in extreme heat, don't be afraid to wear a sunhat.

FULLY PREPARED

The photograph of Arantxa Sanchez shows clearly how modern stars come prepared for matches. A top player will carry a tennis bag on court, which will contain several rackets, extra shirts, a towel, a pair of shoes, all necessary first-aid equipment, tape, and perhaps a

bottle for drinks. Sanchez is carrying rackets, her bag and her sweatsuit top. Note the head and wrist bands.

SHOES

For top players there is a variety of shoes for different court surfaces, such as clay, cement, indoor, grass and so on. My advice is to find a pair that gives you a good fit, has ankle support, is slip-proof and hard-wearing, and suitable for the surface you play on *most* of the time. Ideally, you should have two or three different pairs for various court surfaces.

BASIC GRIPS: THE FOREHAND

Gripping the racket is one of the most important basic skills. The way you do this will influence the angle of the racket face, where you actually meet the ball, and what happens when the strings of the racket contact the ball.

Ever since tennis began, there have been differing views on what grip to use, and this remains a subject of some controversy today. The simple answer is to use the grip that works best for you. If it limits your performance, it should be modified. If you volley with a western forehand grip, you will find it very difficult to hit a low volley because of the angle of the racket face, but if you modify the grip to a chopper grip, this will make it easier to play the shot.

There are three grips that could be described as basic — eastern, continental, and western. The simplest grip for a beginner to master on the forehand is an eastern grip, where the palm of the hand is behind the racket handle.

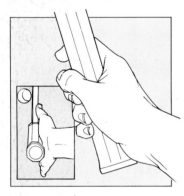

EASTERN FOREHAND GRIP

In this grip, the palm of the hand is behind the racket handle, and it is ideal for balls of varying heights. It is called the shake-hands grip, since it is a natural extension of the hand. To find the grip, place your gripping hand flat on the strings and slide the hand down the handle of the racket until you reach nearly the end of the handle. Then take hold of the racket, as if shaking hands with it.

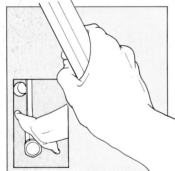

CONTINENTAL GRIP

Used for a variety of shots, this grip requires a strong wrist and more precise timing than the eastern grip. It isn't really recommended for the average player hitting ground strokes. With this grip, the palm of the hand is on top of the racket. When gripping the racket, spread your fingers out a little and ensure that the thumb is wrapped around the racket.

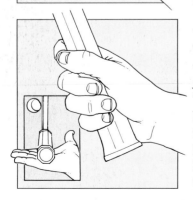

WESTERN FOREHAND GRIP

This is ideal for both high-bouncing, and waist-high balls. The palm of the hand is now underneath the handle of the racket. The grip does make it difficult to hit low-bouncing balls, both on the baseline and at the net, because it is hard to get the racket head down for these low balls. It is, however, ideal for hitting with heavy topspin.

POWERFUL FOREHAND
Ivan Lendl has one of the most powerful forehands in the game. Here he is seen making contact with the ball on the forehand side, using his eastern forehand grip. The palm of his hand is behind the handle of the racket to help achieve maximum strength. This grip is simply a natural extension of the hand.

 STAR TIP

If you want to hit an aggressive forehand with topspin try using a "semi-western" forehand grip. It is often played with the body facing the net for better impact and control.

BASIC GRIPS: THE BACKHAND (1)

A variety of grips can be used on the backhand, depending on whether you play the shot single-handed or double-handed. It is usually a good idea to try the single-handed backhand to start with, but if you have difficulty or feel more comfortable with two hands, then use them.

SINGLE-HANDED BACKHAND
For the single-handed backhand you need to use the basic grip — the eastern backhand grip. This grip can be found by turning your hand a quarter of a turn inwards from the eastern forehand grip so that your knuckle is on top of the racket. The heel of the hand is partly on the left bevel of the racket (if right-handed). Make sure your thumb is positioned diagonally across the back of the handle. This is a strong grip as it provides strength behind the handle, but also allows for a degree of flexibility.

[1] Stefan Edberg has one of the best single-handed backhands on the men's circuit. The palm of his hand is on top of the handle. He has turned the grip inwards from his forehand grip. This helps to provide him with extra strength behind the handle and also a degree of flexibility. This is a sensitive but strong grip, recommended for all beginners. The thumb is positioned diagonally across the racket.

DOUBLE-HANDED BACKHAND

The double-handed backhand (see pages 14-15) is very popular, especially among top players.

2 Chris Evert has one of the best double-handed backhands in the game. Technically she has a very sound shot, which is a model for any budding young player. Notice how her hands are next to each other on the grip and how both arms are working together.

3 & 4 Monica Seles is an unusual player as she hits both forehands and backhands with two hands. She is ambidextrous. Some very young children do this when they take up tennis, primarily when they use a racket which is far too big for them. Monica serves left-handed, so her backhand is quite conventional here. With her forehand, notice how the left hand is at the bottom of the racket.

5 Connors, together with Evert, led the way with two-handed backhands in the 1970s. Many children then started to copy these stars, and the two-handed backhand gained in popularity. Today several of the top players hit with two hands on the backhand.

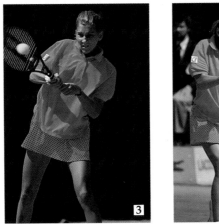

BASIC GRIPS: THE BACKHAND (2)

You may have difficulty playing a one-handed backhand. The easiest way to solve this problem is to add your free hand to the racket (next to the eastern forehand). This converts your backhand into a two-handed backhand, and makes the shot very easy to play as there is no grip change. Both the left and right hands hold the racket with forehand grips.

The advantages of a double-handed backhand include greater strength with two hands rather than one (this is particularly important for the physically weak beginner), and more flexibility and control of the swing. It is also easier to disguise shots using two hands on the racket.

The major disadvantage of using two hands is that it limits your reach. You need to be fast around the court if you play two-handed; you have to get slightly closer to the ball, and the actual hitting area is different from the conventional one-handed backhand.

Most of the top players (e.g. Mats Wilander), will use a backhand grip on their two-handed ground strokes. This makes it easier to hit topspin (see pages 44-45) and also to play a one-handed shot if the need arises. Jimmy Connors, however, is a notable exception. He uses a forehand grip, and consequently hits a very flat or sliced ball.

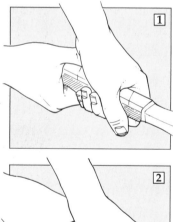

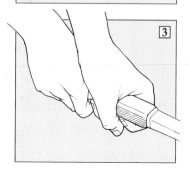

DOUBLE-HANDED

STYLE 1
The beginner often plays a two-handed backhand using a forehand grip with the bottom hand (this is the hand nearest to the end of the handle). The free hand (top hand) is just added to the racket in a forehand grip. This is the easiest way to improve your backhand play.

STYLE 2
Some players only modify the grip with the bottom hand, moving it slightly to a continental grip. Again the free hand grips the racket with a forehand grip.

STYLE 3
Many advanced players change the grip of the bottom hand to a full eastern backhand. This makes it easier to hit the ball with topspin, which many players use as a form of attacking play.

Whatever type of backhand grip you use, the important thing is to feel comfortable with it. Think carefully about the choice of grip in practice, so that during a game you can use your chosen grip naturally.

SLOWER SURFACES
André Agassi, who is often seen wearing denim jeans, has a very effective two-handed backhand. Notice how he has both hands close to each other on the grip, and how he has taken the racket back below the height of the ball, so that he can readily lift the ball back or hit it with topspin. Agassi uses his two-handed backhand to great effect, particularly on slower surfaces.

 STAR TIP
If you plan to play a double-handed backhand, I recommend a grip change to the eastern backhand. When you practice it is also a good idea to hit some one-handed shots as well, in case you need them in a match.

THE FOREHAND DRIVE

1

2

4

1 The forehand drive is the most fundamental shot in tennis, and once it is mastered, you are almost ready to play a game. The easiest grip to use is the eastern forehand. Start from the ready position – this is the position from which it is easiest for you to get off the mark, so that you can get into the right position at the right time to hit the ball.

In the ready position, the racket is held out in front of the body in the forehand grip. It is supported by the free hand at the throat (unless two-handed). Stand with your feet shoulder-width apart, knees bent and springy, with your body weight bent toward the racket. Your eyes should be focused on your opponent and the ball. The ready position for your ground strokes is approximately 1 yard (1m) behind the center mark on the baseline. A beginner may well stand inside the baseline. Martina Navratilova is in an ideal ready position here – note the low body position.

2 – **4** From this position take the racket back as soon as you see the ball leave your opponent's racket and come to your forehand side. This is done by turning at the hips and shoulders. The backswing doesn't need to be very long or very high, and should be in the form of a small loop. The height of the racket takeback will depend largely on the height of the oncoming ball. At this moment, your weight is on your back foot.

[5]

[9]

[5] You then need a smooth connection between the back-swing and the forward swing. This swing is from low to high, giving the ball lift. As the racket comes forward, your weight is transferred to your front foot. The racket finishes in a high position and in the direction that you want the ball to go. Use your free hand for balance.

[6]

[6] – [8] The key to hitting a good forehand is the "hitting area" or "contact point" with the ball. This needs to be in front of the leading hip, and at a comfortable distance away from the body. Your grip needs to be very firm on contact with the ball. Stay balanced throughout the shot.

[10]

[11]

[7]

[8]

[9] – [11] For the beginner, the easiest level at which to hit the ball is between knee and waist height. Initially you will find it easier to hit a falling ball, i.e. to strike the ball as it is falling after the top of the bounce. The arc of a falling ball often tends to encourage the correct grooved action on the forward swing.

It would be very difficult for an absolute beginner to try to pay attention to all these points at once. It is much simpler to think of TURN, STEP, and SWING. By turning the body the racket is taken back. By stepping you transfer your weight forward, and by swinging from low to high with the racket you are able to hit the ball.

If a "semi-western" grip is used, when the weight is transferred forward the stance will be semi-open (even more open if a full western grip is used). The hitting area will be level with the front foot, but still a comfortable distance away from the body. It is easier to hit high-bouncing balls with this grip, but far more difficult with low balls.

THE BACKHAND DRIVE – ONE-HANDED

1

2

3

[1] For the beginner the one-handed backhand is often a difficult shot to master. Start in the ready position (the same position you use with the forehand). As soon as you see the ball coming to your backhand side, change your grip to an eastern backhand.

[2] Then turn early at the hips and shoulders to get a good shoulder turn for the backhand. Make sure that your racket is supported

with your free hand as you take it back. This hand only comes off the racket just before impact.

[3] Now transfer your weight onto your front foot by stepping into the shot. Make sure you step forward and not parallel with the baseline.

[4] The backswing is connected to the forward swing by a shallow loop in a low-to-high action, giving the feeling of lift on the backhand.

[5] The hitting area or contact point is slightly in front of the leading foot, again at a comfortable distance from the body. The grip is firm on impact. As I mentioned in the forehand section, it is much easier for a beginner to hit the ball between knee and waist height, and to hit it as it starts to fall after reaching the top of the bounce.

[6] – [8] The follow-through is high and in the direction that you want the ball to go. Try to maintain your balance throughout the shot. On completion of the stroke, return to the ready position.

THE BACKHAND DRIVE – TWO-HANDED

1 Both the very young and the physically small player may find this shot easier to master initially than the one-handed backhand, because two hands will provide more strength.

This shot has the same preparation as the one-handed shot except that both hands are now next to each other, on the grip, as shown here by Monica Seles. Start from the ready position. For variations of grips see pages 14-15.

2 Turn at the shoulders and hips as soon as you see the ball coming to your backhand.

3 Now transfer your weight forward onto your front foot. The hitting area with two hands tends to be level with your front hip, but needs to be a comfortable distance away from the body (slightly closer than for a one-handed backhand). If you are too close to the ball, the shot becomes cramped and it is difficult to get a proper swing.

4 & 5 The follow-through is high and in front of the body, sometimes even finishing over the shoulder. The arms are not tucked into the body, as this would cramp the shot.

If you are undecided whether to use two hands or just one hand, it is a good idea to decide whether you are simply copying another player or whether it is a natural stroke for you. Don't forget that if you play two-handed you need to be able to move quickly around the court. If you are equally good with one and two hands, try to gauge how fast you are. If you aren't particularly quick, you would be better off hitting one-handed.

Likewise, a player who is not very strong physically might get more balls over the net using two hands rather than just one hand.

6 – 10 Mary-Joe Fernandez, runner-up in the 1990 Australian Open, is seen in this sequence hitting a very effective two-handed backhand – a model for right-handed players.

THE SERVICE (1)

The service is one of the most important shots in the game. It is also the only shot that you have complete mastery over, since you toss the ball in the air and *you* hit it.

As soon as you have a little skill, you must try to master the overarm serve. Here the ball is tossed in the air, and struck while above your head.

To start with, you will tend to use the forehand grip on the service. Initially, the main aim is to get the ball over the net and into the correct area, with a simple "throwing" action.

First, take up a stance behind the baseline in a sideways position. Your front foot should be pointing slightly toward the net post, and your back foot should be parallel with the baseline. Place your feet about shoulder-width apart. Whatever position you adopt, make sure it is comfortable and suits you. In a singles match it is a good idea to stand near the center mark, as this position represents the shortest distance between you and your opponent's service box (ideal for hitting a flat serve down the center line). In doubles, you need to stand about halfway between the center mark and the singles sideline.

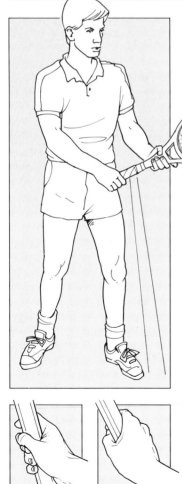

THE READY POSITION
Stand with your feet shoulder-width apart in a comfortable sideways position behind the baseline. Start with the racket and ball together, pointing roughly to the service box that you are aiming for.

THE GRIP
To begin, use your accustomed forehand grip. This can be used as a service grip while you are trying to master the basic action.

IMPROVING YOUR SERVICE
Once you have the basic action, it is vital to progress to the more flexible continental (or chopper) grip. The more a player uses the forehand grip, the more ingrained it becomes and the harder it is to change. In the initial stages of using the continental grip, you will find that the ball tends to slice out to the side. This is because the angle of the racket face on impact with the ball is now slightly different. To help to get a flatter serve, either bring your shoulder around more, or turn your wrist slightly, prior to impact with the ball. There are many facets to the serve, and it is a good idea to concentrate on only one at a time as you try to improve.

BECKER
Boris Becker is positioned behind the baseline with his feet a comfortable space apart. The ball and racket are together. The racket is pointing in the direction of the service box. This is a good stance from which to begin.

THE SERVICE (2)

1 Start from the ready position (see page 22), with the ball and racket together pointing toward the box you are aiming for. Hold the ball in your fingertips. Try to start in a relaxed manner, with your weight slightly forward.

2 – 4 Both arms must work rhythmically together. As the racket is taken out at the back, the left arm starts to come upward and releases the ball. Both arms go down and out as the shoulders open up.

5 & 6 The ball is placed high in the air. It is easier to place the ball above your outstretched reach and hit it as it is falling, than to hit the ball as it is rising (this requires precise timing and is very difficult for the beginner). Toss the ball a comfortable distance in front and slightly to the right of the body (if right-handed; to the left of the body if left-handed). In order to get a good toss, try to release the ball when your arm is straight and in front of your body. Don't forget: you do not have to hit a bad toss — leave it and toss the ball up again.

7 The racket drops down onto the back. Note the knee bend, so that the player can use his leg strength to drive up to the ball.

9

10

11

8 Here the racket has dropped down onto the back. Notice the high elbow position. From here the racket head is "thrown up" at the ball (without, of course, letting go of the racket!) as the player extends upwards.

9 The racket is now thrown up at the ball. In order to generate pace on the serve, the racket head needs to come through quickly.

The player might now be off the ground. If you have difficulty with the throwing action, try practicing over-arm throws with a tennis ball until you can throw the ball from one baseline to the other. Contact with the ball is made at the player's maximum reach. The wrist is firm but flexible.

10 & **11** The racket follows through in the direction of the ball, ending on the left side of the body (for a right-hander). As the racket comes through, the player lands inside the court, having maintained good balance throughout the stroke. From here you need to return to the ready position.

THE RETURN OF SERVE

If the service is the most important shot in the game, then the return of service is the second most important.

The main aim of the return of service is to get the ball back over the net and into play. Don't worry about trying to hit the cover off the ball: chip it, chop it, block it — but whatever you do, force your opponent to hit another ball after the serve. Once the return is in play, you increase your chance of winning the point.

Position yourself properly for the return of service. If your opponent has a weak service, move forward. If the server has a powerful service, stand further back and just block the return. Try to pick up the ball *early*. This is done by watching the ball carefully. Try to find clues as to where your opponent is going to serve by watching the server and the ball during the service action.

As a beginner, the most important point is to be alert on your toes. As the server tosses the ball in the air, get ready to move. Check when the server strikes the ball, and then move forward to hit the return.

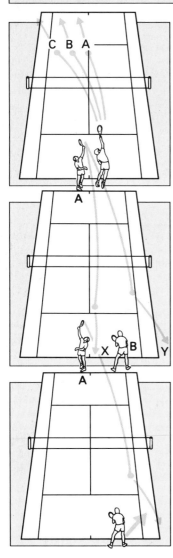

SERVICE POSITIONS
The server has the choice of where to position the ball in the service box:
1) either serve hard and flat down the center line (A);
2) or to a position (B) straight at the opponent, or sliced into the opponent's body;
3) or to position (C), i.e. sliced out wide (for a right-hander).

POSITION OF RECEIVER
The receiver has to concentrate very hard when receiving serve, and needs to stand in the middle of the serving angle. The server can hit the ball anywhere between the two lines X and Y.
A server B receiver

MOVE EARLY FOR A WIDE BALL
One of the hardest serves for the beginner to return is the *wide* sliced serve or the high-kicking topspin serve. The key to returning these difficult serves is to move *forward* and take the ball *early* . If you move into the ball, you should be able to take it before it has bounced high (topspin) or before it has cut away (slice).

When returning the wide serve, try to follow the path of the arrows, as shown here in the diagram.
A server

GOOD RETURN OF SERVE
Jimmy Connors in his heyday was renowned for the quality of his returns of service. He had the ability to pick the ball up early, and invariably attacked the return. Notice how even when slightly off the ground Connors is leaning into the shot to attack this backhand return.

 STAR
TIP
A good server can hit the ball in many different ways. The receiver must be flexible and capable of hitting the ball from many different positions.

THE FOREHAND VOLLEY

A volley is any shot which is played before the ball bounces. It is generally played from near to the net. Technically, the volley is the simplest shot to teach.

If you are a beginner, the easiest grip to use is the basic eastern forehand grip; however, as you progress it is preferable to use the chopper or continental grip because you can use this for both the forehand and backhand volleys.

When you are at the net, it is quite common to have to face a succession of forehand and backhand volleys, and it is far more convenient to use one grip for all your volley shots. Net play often involves split-second timing, allowing little opportunity to change the grip. Once you have mastered the basics, you will find that the chopper or continental grip is the best to use.

STEP 1

Start from the ready position, approximately 6–8ft (1.82–2.44m) from the net. (Hint: touch the net with your racket and then move back two paces.) You are now much nearer to your opponent, so be alert in a springy position, and ready to move. Hold the racket out in front of you, supported at the throat by your free hand. Watch your opponent and the ball carefully – this will help you to decide which side the ball is coming. As soon as your opponent strikes the ball, check. This enables you to get your weight evenly distributed, and to push off to whichever side the ball comes.

STEP 2

Prepare early with a short takeback, and then contact the ball well out in front of you, at a comfortable distance from your body. Your arm will be slightly bent. The action is a PUNCHING or BLOCKING one. Let the racket do the work with very little follow-through.

In order to get some power into the volley as you move forward to the ball, transfer your weight onto your front foot; step into the shot.

STEP 3

Try to keep the follow-through short so that you will have time to get ready for the next shot. The volleyer should have a very firm wrist on contact. Notice how balanced the volleyer is.

POSITIONING
Mats Wilander is seen here moving forward to hit his forehand volley. His eyes are focused on the ball, the racket head is up and he is transferring his weight onto his front foot. The wrist is very firm. Wilander is going to hit this volley well out in front of his body – excellent positioning.

 STAR TIP
Hold the racket well out in front of you and always try to meet the ball early. Power and control are obtained from weight transfer and timing, not by swinging the racket head – always PUNCH or BLOCK the ball.

THE BACKHAND VOLLEY

he backhand volley can be played either with one hand or with two hands. First, let us take a closer look at the one-handed backhand volley.

You should start from the ready position with the chopper (or backhand) grip mentioned previously. The racket takeback is very short (like the forehand volley), but this time the supporting free hand only comes off the racket just before the ball makes contact with the racket strings.

The racket is brought forward in a PUNCHING or BLOCKING action. The ball is contacted well out in front of the body, at a comfortable distance to the side. Again, power is obtained by transferring the weight forward, so try to step into the shot. Remember to keep the follow-through short for a solid volley.

The two-handed backhand volley has the same action as that of the one-hander, although generally the takeback is slightly longer. Be careful not to swing at the volley if you use two hands. The hands must be close together on the grip. Beginners may get more strength on the backhand volley with two hands.

CONTROL
When Stefan Edberg won the men's title at Wimbledon in 1988, he proved that one of his most successful shots was his backhand volley. Edberg shows perfect control as he steps forward to this backhand volley. The racket is supported with his left hand at the throat. His arm is straight, the wrist firm. He has good weight transference to get power into the volley. Notice the concentration on his face as he strikes the ball. If you hit volleys like this, you will have a lot of success!

 STAR TIP
When volleying one-handed, always use your free hand to support the racket. Keep volleying well out in front of your body. Be positive and go to meet the ball. Remember: volleying is fun.

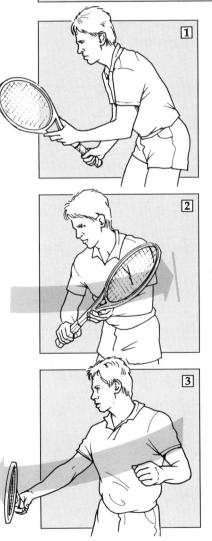

STEP 1
The ready position – use either a chopper or backhand grip. As for all shots, you need to be alert and on your toes. This is especially important if playing close to the net – particularly in doubles.

STEP 2
Here the racket is supported with the free hand as it is taken back. Note the short takeback. This is an advantage if you are close to the net and have little time to prepare for your shot.

STEP 3
The action is then a short punch or block with little follow-through. Note how the weight is going forward to get power into the shot. The grip must be firm on impact, and good balance must be maintained throughout the stroke. After hitting the ball, recover quickly to the ready position for the next shot.

The three steps show the one-handed backhand volley. Although you can use a two-handed volley, the major disadvantage is one of reach. This means you need to be quicker on your feet and you also need to use a slightly longer backswing. It is advisable to play one-handed volleys whenever possible.

VOLLEY VARIATIONS (1)

In addition to the basic volley, you may have to play *half-volleys*, *high volleys* and *low volleys*.

You might be forced to play the *half-volley* when you are coming into the net, but haven't moved quite quickly enough. The ball is played just after the bounce, at about ground level. It is a shot you might play instinctively, but really it is a defensive shot, played when you are out of position. It needs good footwork and balance if it is to be executed properly. To play this shot you need to get down to the ball, so bend your knees and take a short back-swing to come forward with a low-to-high action. Follow through in the direction you want the ball to go. The racket face is slightly open on impact, and the grip and the wrist are firm.

The *high volley* may look easy to hit, but all too often a player swings at the ball, with the result that the ball ends up over the baseline. The key is to watch the ball very carefully, set yourself up to play the volley with a high racket takeback, and then exaggerate the high-to-low volleying action, while playing the ball well out in front of the body.

The *low volley* is often one of the most difficult volleys to play, as the ball is coming low over the net and you are forced to hit it upward to get it back over the net. It is played generally when you are a long way from the net and your opponent has hit a good return at your feet.

There are four basic points to remember when hitting a low volley: bend your knees, not your back; open the racket face so that it is tilted back slightly; keep the racket head up; and play the ball out in front of you.

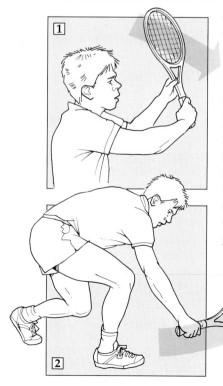

THE HIGH BACKHAND VOLLEY

The racket is taken back above shoulder height. The action is a high-to-low one; the follow-through is short.

THE LOW BACKHAND VOLLEY

Notice the low position of the player. The racket head is up and the racket face slightly open. The ball is struck well out in front of the body and the follow-through is then slightly upward, to help lift the ball over the net and deep into the opponent's court. If necessary, sacrifice some pace to get a good length.

TECHNICAL POINTS
This photograph highlights the main technical points on the low volley. Tim Mayotte, who has a strong serve-and-volley game, gets down low to the volley. His knees are bent, the racket face is slightly open, and the racket head is up. Tim is about to contact the ball out in front of the body. The low volley is hard to play, but Tim makes it look easy.

 STAR
TIP
Try to get into the net quickly so you don't have to play half-volleys.

VOLLEY VARIATIONS (2)

The other variations on the volley include the *drop volley*, the *drive volley* and the *lob volley*.

The *drop volley* is similar to the drop shot, except that it is played before the ball bounces. Generally it is played when the ball is at, or below, net height. This shot requires a great deal of touch and feel for the ball. You need a short backswing and reduced follow-through for this shot. Make sure your wrist is firm on impact, and that the racket face is open to help impart more backspin on to the ball. Try to keep your eye on the ball, your head over the ball, and bend your knees.

The *drive volley* is sometimes used as an approach shot. It is hit from the mid-court area and, as its name suggests, it is a combination of a drive and volley, with the characteristics of both. Use a longer backswing than for a normal volley. In order to control the shot, it is advisable to hit the ball with a little topspin.

The *lob volley* is more common in doubles than in singles. It is particularly effective when all four players are at the net and it is used as a surprise, forcing the opposing pair to retreat to the baseline. It is similar to the basic lob (see pages 38-39), but is played before the ball bounces. This shot requires a fine touch. If played badly, it can have drastic consequences, particularly if it gives your opponent an easy smash!

HIGH BACKHAND DRIVE VOLLEY

Jimmy Connors is seen in full flight playing a high drive volley on the back-hand side. Connors often uses drive volleys when coming into the net as approach shots. Here he is about to contact the ball, even with his feet well off the ground. Notice how he is balanced and poised even in this position, and how his eyes are clearly focused on the ball. This is a difficult shot to control for the beginner.

FOREHAND DROP VOLLEY

If played effectively, a good drop volley lands short in your opponent's court (i.e. just over the net); the backspin makes the ball stay low. Tactically it is useful as an element of surprise, particularly if your opponent is standing well behind the base-line. It is, however, a relatively difficult shot to master.

FOREHAND DRIVE VOLLEY

This stroke can be used against a slow, high-bouncing ball when close to the net; against high balls when coming into the net; or, alternatively, to introduce an element of surprise, by moving off the base-line quickly and not allowing a floating return to bounce.

FOREHAND LOB VOLLEY

This shot is used mainly as a surprise, when your opponent is very close to the net. If played effectively, it can open up the court for a better range of angled shots. Hit the ball in front, giving it sufficient height by opening up the racket face and getting an upward follow-through.

THE SMASH

The smash is very much like the serve – with the same throwing action.

For beginners, the smash is a hard shot to master. The key to success is good footwork and good positioning, so make sure that you spend plenty of time getting your footwork right. Move as quickly as possible to get underneath the ball on the smash. Try to get back to the ball in a sideways movement, and position yourself so that the ball is in front and slightly to the right of the body (for a right-hander).

Once in the smashing position, really *throw* the racket head up at the ball. Pick your target area on court and go for it, don't just pat the ball back. Make sure you complete the stroke with a good follow-through in the direction of the ball and then recover to the ready position – you might get another lob!

It is also possible to hit a backhand smash, but this is a difficult shot to do properly. It is better to run around the ball and play the forehand smash (good footwork is required) because you have less power with the backhand smash.

If you are forced to play the backhand smash, really turn the right shoulder (if right-handed) around behind the ball, to enable you to throw the racket up and over the ball.

Less power, and greater accuracy, are the two key elements to remember.

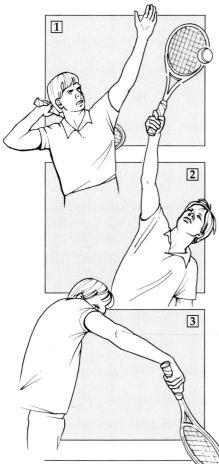

STEP 1
Having started from the ready position, take the racket straight on to your back. Position yourself in a sideways stance. Point your free hand at the ball to help your balance, and keep your eyes focused on the ball.

STEP 2
The racket head is then thrown up at the ball, and the point of impact with the ball should be at your maximum reach. Good players will move back quickly for difficult smashes, and may even play these with their feet off the ground.

STEP 3
Like the service, it is essential to have a good follow-through. Snapping your wrist over after contacting the ball helps to bring the ball down. Sometimes you might prefer to smash the ball after the bounce. This is a good idea from a high lob on a windy day, or when the sun is shining directly into your eyes, making it difficult for you to see the ball.

OVERHEAD SMASH
*Boris Becker is physically a very strong player and has a powerful overhead shot. He has jumped off the ground to play this smash. Becker uses the strength in his arm and wrist to bring the racket over on the follow-through. He has taken off on one foot, and will land on the other. There are basically two types of smash: the **offensive smash** which is hit from close to the net for a winner; and the **defensive smash** hit from a deep lob, possibly for a winner, but more often just to keep you in the point. Becker attempts to make this an offensive smash.*

 STAR TIP
Make sure you get underneath the ball. To judge your positioning, allow the ball to bounce when practicing. If you are in the correct position it will bounce just in front of you.

THE LOB

The lob is perhaps the most underrated shot in the game, but if played effectively and at the right time, it can be a match-winning shot. A lob can be either a defensive shot, played when under pressure and in trouble, or an attacking shot, when played with topspin against an aggressive volleyer.

A defensive lob (A) is generally hit from behind the baseline or when you are stretched wide out of court for a ball. The aim here is to put the ball up high, in order to give yourself time to recover your position.

An offensive lob (B) is hit lower and generally from inside the baseline. The aim is to hit the ball just high enough so that it is out of the reach of your opponent (allowing for a jump as well), but not so high that the player has time to turn and chase the ball.

THE FOREHAND LOB SEQUENCE OF SHOTS
The lob is very much a touch shot, so try to hit it gently into the air so that you can control the height and length that you hit the ball.

1 READY POSITION
The forehand lob is played in a similar way to the forehand drive, with two notable exceptions. Start in the ready position.

2 EARLY PREPARATION
Take the racket back early, as soon as you see the ball coming to your forehand side.

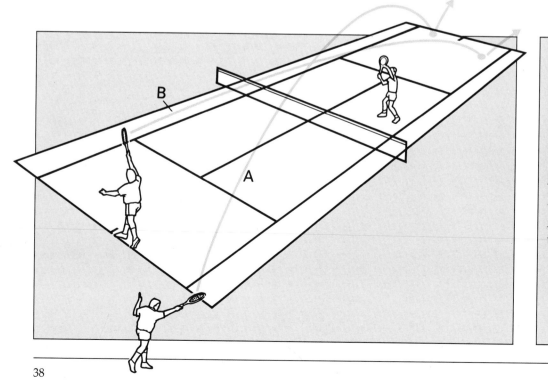

THE BACKHAND LOB SEQUENCE
The backhand lob is played in a similar fashion. Use the basic backhand grip. The racket swings down and under the ball at impact, with the racket face open. Again, the follow-through is high.

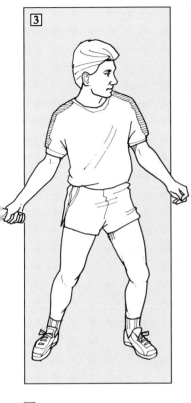

3 RACKET COMING
  FORWARD
Then make a smooth con-
nection between the back-
swing and forward swing.

4 OPEN RACKET FACE
The swing is from low to
high, and on impact the
racket face must be slightly
open.

5 HIT IN FRONT
The racket comes from
below the ball. The ball is hit
in front of the body and at a
comfortable distance to the
side of the body. The body
weight is transferred
forward.

6 FOLLOW-THROUGH
The follow-through is then
slightly higher than that for
a normal forehand drive.

THE DROP SHOT

At junior level the drop shot is perhaps the most under-used shot, yet if you play it at the correct time, you can easily win the point outright. The aim is to hit the ball with sufficient backspin to make it land as near to the net as possible. With a great deal of backspin, the ball will die as it hits the ground. The beginner should try to concentrate on getting the ball to bounce as near to the net as possible. Drop shots can be hit anywhere in the court, but the further back the shot is played, the more risky it becomes.

Unless you possess a good touch, and certainly at beginner level, it is advisable to play the drop shot from an offensive position, in or around the service box.

The key to a good drop shot is deception, so try to prepare for your drop shot as you would for a normal forehand or backhand drive, and remember — only play the drop shot when you are moving forward to the ball.

THE FOREHAND DROP SHOT

READY POSITION
The racket is taken back at about shoulder height (as for the normal forehand drive) and the player starts to move toward the ball.

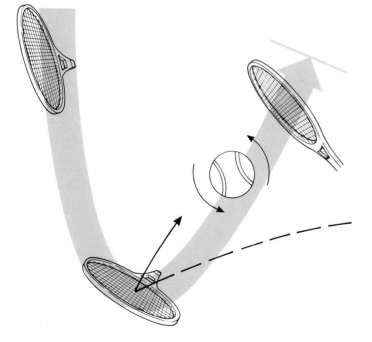

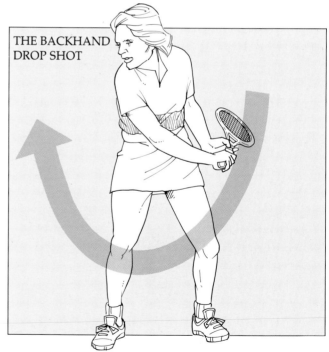

THE BACKHAND DROP SHOT

READY POSITION
Again, start from the ready position and change your grip to an eastern backhand grip. Take the racket back high, and support it with your free hand. If disguised, it should look as if you are going to slice the ball.

The drop shot takes a lot of experience and practice to perfect. The easiest drop shot to play is one down the line, as the ball has to travel the shortest distance. For a beginner, a bad cross-court drop shot at least has the advantage of taking the opponent out of court, whereas a bad down-the-line drop shot could be put away for a winner. Have fun trying the drop shot.

MEETING THE BALL
The racket then comes down and underneath the ball with an open racket face, imparting backspin on the ball. The shape of the swing is similar to the letter C.

FOLLOW-THROUGH
The follow-through is slightly upward. The drop shot can be used to tire your opponent; to break up your opponent's rhythm; to bring a baseliner into the net; as an element of surprise; or against a weak second serve.

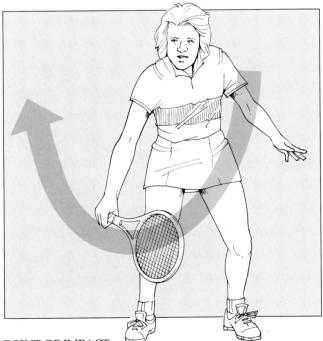

POINT OF IMPACT
Step into the ball and bring the racket down in a C shape. The point of impact is in front of the body, and the racket face is slightly open. The racket then comes down and underneath the ball, imparting backspin on the ball.

FOLLOW-THROUGH
Try to have a good follow-through, with the racket finishing slightly upward in the direction that you want the ball to go. In early learning stages, don't worry if the ball clears the net by a reasonable margin — it is better to improve your control of backspin than try to get the ball to skim the net.

USE OF SPIN ON THE GROUND STROKES

Now that you have mastered the basics on the forehand and backhand drives, it is time to see how you can vary these shots.

One way to do this is to put spin on the ball. This could be by topspin — when you make the ball kick up and go high — or by slice, when you make the ball skid and stay low. You could also use sidespin, making the ball curve to the left or right, and moving it away from your opponent.

Modern players tend to hit with topspin. The ball spins from low to high on a vertical axis, causing downward force so that the path of the ball is like the arch of a rainbow. Topspin can be used from the baseline, to allow you to hit the ball higher over the net for safety (the spin will cause the ball to dip). You can then hit an aggressive shot without any fear of making an error, as most of the power is turned into spin.

Topspin can also be used as a passing shot. In this case, it is hit lower over the net. The advantage is that the spin will cause the ball to dip. This means that you can hit it directly at the oncoming player's feet.

STEP 1
Racket head comes from below the ball
Topspin is easy to learn. Start from the ready position. Prepare as for a normal forehand drive, but bring the racket head down much lower than for a normal forehand drive, at least 1 ft (30cm) below the intended point of impact. The key to a successful topspin shot is *where the racket comes from*, so make sure that you can bring the racket upward, towards the sky.

STEP 2   Point of impact
The racket face is closed and the ball is struck in a low-to-high swing, with the racket approaching a vertical position to the ground on impact. In fact, if you started with the racket touching the ground and then just lifted the racket up, keeping the face vertical, the ball would have topspin on it.

STEP 3   Follow-through
The more spin you want on the ball, the more the racket needs to travel in a 6 to 12 o'clock direction. Follow through over the ball with a long, smooth finish. Many players who hit with excessive topspin have an extreme follow-through, where the body really swings around.

HEAVY TOPSPIN
Gabriela Sabatini hits her forehand with heavy topspin. This extreme follow-through is typical of players hitting with a lot of topspin. Notice how her body has swung around on the follow-through, and how the shot has been hit with an open stance.

INSET
Here Mikael Pernfors shows how the racket head comes from below the ball when hitting with topspin.

STAR TIP
The most suitable grip to use for heavy topspin is the semi-western or western forehand grip. You will often find it easier with a semi-open stance.

USE OF TOPSPIN ON THE BACKHAND

The use of topspin increased after the successes of Bjorn Borg in the late 1970s. Borg used phenomenal topspin off both the forehand and backhand sides. Slow courts, particularly clay, are most suited to topspin because of their high bounce. Many tournaments are played on clay, so it is wise to have topspin in your range of shots.

Once you have mastered the topspin forehand, have a go on the backhand side as well. This shot is played in a similar fashion to the forehand. In fact, if you are two-handed you might even find that it is easier than the forehand, and that it comes naturally to you on this side. Start in the ready position, and change your grip to an eastern backhand.

Even if you are two-handed, try to use an eastern backhand grip, as this is better for imparting spin to the ball.

STEP 1   Lower takeback
Once you have an eastern backhand grip, turn early at the shoulders. Even if you initially take the racket back high (like Becker) make sure that the racket head comes down well below the ball. The racket is supported with the free hand on the takeback. This helps to give you more control and also helps to make you more aware of the racket face.

STEP 2   Angle of racket-face
Transfer your weight forward onto the front foot as you prepare to make contact with the ball. The racket face is closed slightly on impact, while the racket head is brought vertically up the back of the ball and forward to generate power. The more the racket head is accelerated through the stroke, the more power and momentum are achieved. Remember to contact the ball in front of your body.

STEP 3   Follow-through
Follow through high and in the direction of the target. If you have difficulty hitting with topspin, check that the angle of the racket face is correct on impact (if it is too closed, the ball ends up in the bottom of the net). Also check that the racket head is coming from well below the ball (this is essential if you are to get sufficient spin on the ball); that you are preparing early enough; that the grip is right and your stance not too closed.

HEAVY TOPSPIN
Michael Chang hits with heavy topspin on his two-handed backhand. He is seen holding the racket with a backhand grip, and the racket head is coming from well below the ball. This makes it easy for him to brush up the back of the ball and impart spin to it.

 STAR TIP
The key to good topspin is to bring the racket well below the ball on the back-swing.

THE SLICE BACKHAND

The slice is generally hit on the backhand side. Some players use it on the forehand as well, against high-bouncing balls or as a last resort when badly out of position. If played defensively, it is hit from the baseline and is often used when a player is not in a good position to play an attacking backhand. It can also be used effectively to change the pace and direction of the ball.

If you use the slice offensively, then it is played as an approach shot, for instance, when your opponent has hit a short ball and you want to play a shot and come into the net. The ball is hit low over the net; on bouncing it will stay low, forcing your opponent to lift the ball in order to get it back over the net. This will, in turn, give you an easier volley.

The slice is difficult to play two-handed because the second hand limits the follow-through. You will find that many players who normally hit two-handed tend to slice with one hand. Other players start with two hands and let the second hand come off on the follow-through.

STEP 1 Takeback for slice

Start in the ready position and then change your grip to an eastern backhand. If you use a forehand grip, the angle of the racket face will be too open on impact and the ball will sail up into the air. As soon as you see the ball coming to your backhand side, turn at the hips and shoulders and take the racket back high, above the level of the oncoming ball.

STEP 2 Impact

Keep the wrist firm and then bite into the ball with a high-to-low swing. The racket face will be slightly open on impact. The ball is hit in front of the body and at a comfortable distance to the side. Note how the player's body is leaning forward into the shot. If the angle of the racket is too open on impact with the ball, it will go too high in the air; conversely, if the angle is too closed, the ball will end up in the bottom of the net.

STEP 3 Follow-through

The follow-through should be smooth and out in front of the body. Let the momentum of the shot carry you into the net. To generate more backspin and get the ball to skid, you might find it better to use a shortened follow-through.

HIGH TAKEBACK
Zina Garrison uses her slice to good effect on the backhand. She has a high takeback, and the racket face is slightly open. This will enable her to put a lot of backspin on the ball as she swings through. Zina has an unusually high grip position on her racket handle which suits her game and enables her to get more control with the racket.

STAR TIP
If you are using the slice as an approach shot, try to hit the ball straight rather than cross-court (as you then leave yourself vulnerable for any easy passing shot). You must hit to a good length, i.e. near to the baseline, to force your opponent to hit a difficult passing shot from behind the baseline.

USE OF SPIN ON THE SERVE – TOPSPIN

There are three basic types of serve that you can hit – *flat*, *topspin* (or kick) and *slice*. A good serve is a combination of speed, placement and variation of spin. The server should always keep his opponent guessing as to where the serve is going. Don't forget, if you keep holding your serve, you cannot lose the game except in a tie break; this will keep the pressure on your opponent.

Topspin is the safest serve to use and, because of this, it is popular for second serves as well as first serves. Topspin is also useful on slow, high-bouncing courts, such as cement or clay, where the court surface automatically diminishes the power of the shot.

Imparting spin to the ball with the serve is similar to using topspin on ground strokes. You need to learn a combination of body and racket movements.

SECOND SERVE

The topspin serve is often used as a second serve because it is a safe serve. It is hit higher over the net, reducing the possibility of serving into the net. The spin helps to bring the ball down, reducing the chance of serving the ball long.

Boris Becker is seen poised with a good knee bend, ready to strike the ball in a left-to-right action.

STAR TIP

In the learning stages, try placing the ball further to the left (if right-handed) and slightly behind you, to help you to impart spin to it.

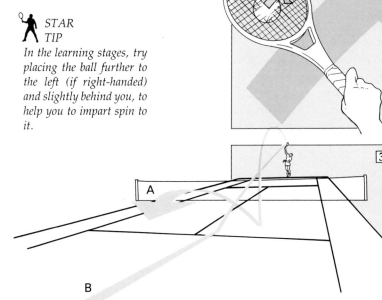

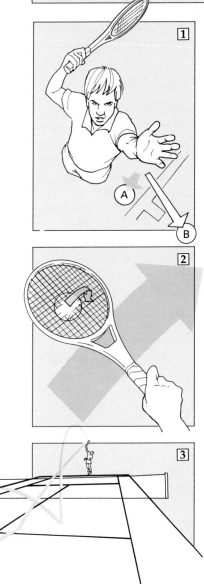

STEP 1 Ball placement

Start in the ready position for the serve with a continental (or backhand) grip. Toss the ball a little to your left (if right-handed). If you let the ball drop onto the ground, it will land slightly to your left. For the beginner it is easier if the ball lands behind you. Once you have the feeling of topspinning the ball, place it to the left, but in front of, the baseline. You will have to arch your back to hit the serve – especially if you are tossing the ball slightly behind you.

A topspin B flat

STEP 2 Racket path

The ball is then struck from left to right. The continental or backhand grip gives greater flexibility of the wrist, and also ensures that the racket face strikes the ball at the correct angle to get ball rotation. Try to use lots of wrist movement and throw the racket head upward, through and past the ball.

STEP 3 Serve paths

The ball travels high over the net on the topspin serve, and the spin then brings it down. On landing, the ball will kick up and outward – making it difficult to return, particularly if hit to the backhand side of your opponent. He will have to play a high, shoulder-height ball, or take the serve very early.

A topspin B flat

USE OF SPIN ON THE SERVE – SLICE

The slice can be used for a first service or a second service, and is played in the same way as a flat service, except that the racket now comes around the side of the ball.

A right-hander serving from the right (deuce) court can make the ball break off to his opponent's right, taking him out of court and forcing a weak return. Likewise, a left-hander such as Martina Navratilova, serving from the left (advantage) court, can make the ball break to her opponent's left and take her out of court.

This technique is particularly effective when a left-hander plays a right-hander, as the ball is traveling away from the right-hander's backhand side. It is also effective on fast surfaces, such as grass.

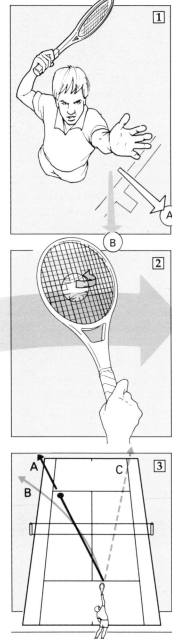

STEP 1   Ball placement
Start in the service ready position with a continental (or backhand) grip. If you are right-handed, place the ball slightly further to your right, but still in front of the body.
A slice B flat

STEP 2   Impact position
Brush around the side of the ball – imagine you are hitting past the ball at three o'clock to impart spin to it. Many players find this easier with a backhand grip. Try some serves with the continental grip and some with the backhand grip to see what suits you best. Your body naturally turns when you serve, so make use of this when slicing the ball. Ensure your wrist is fairly loose to help generate a natural snapping action on impact, and follow through in the normal way.

STEP 3   Effect of slice serve on court
Once the ball bounces it will stay low and break off to the side. This is a good serve to use to make your opponent stretch, and when served wide it can open up the court for a volley. It can be devastating if there is a side wind from the same direction. On grass, a short, angled slice serve is particularly useful if your opponent is a long way behind the baseline.
A flat serve
B slice serve (this draws the receiver out of position and opens up space for the server's first ground stroke)
C ground stroke

SLICE SERVICE
Jimmy Connors, who is left-handed, has a very effective slice service from the left court which takes his opponent well out of court when he uses it against a right-hander. Here, Connors is in full flight. The racket has left his back and he is about to strike the ball, brushing around the side of it and imparting spin to it.

 STAR TIP
In the initial stages of learning, place the ball further to the side, making it easier to impart spin to the ball.

DOUBLES – SIMPLE TACTICS

Most club players play far more doubles than singles. This is partly because the game of doubles is more sociable than singles, partly because it is less energetic (the load is shared between two of you), and also because it is stimulating, involving touch, creativity, imagination and teamwork.

The aim of the game of doubles, and the easiest way to win, is to play from the net. The serving team starts with a tremendous advantage, as they already have one player at the net. If the server follows his serve into the net, this team will be in a dominating position.

At low levels, one-up, one-back, formations are often seen, and there is a lot of cross-court rallying. Try to be adventurous and get to the net, as it is far easier to win points there. Some of the most exciting points played in tennis are between two attacking doubles partnerships – both at the net!

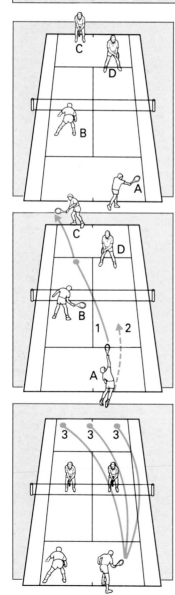

BASIC POSITIONS FOR DOUBLES

The traditional formation for doubles is with the server (A) standing midway between the center mark and the inner sideline. The server's partner (B) stands in the middle of the service box, in the volleying position near the net; the receiver (C) stands near the baseline, but in a position to cover all the possible angles of the serve; and the receiver's partner (D) stands on the service line.

SERVE AND VOLLEY

In doubles, a lot of serves are hit down the center line. If you (A), serve wide, you will open the court up, but give your opponent a greater angle for return. Try to serve a three-quarter pace serve (1) to allow you time to get into the net (2). The receiver (C) and his partner (D) have the option of returning cross-court at your feet; down the middle of the court between you and your partner (B); down the tramline; or of lobbing your partner.

A TYPICAL DOUBLES SITUATION

Here is a typical situation with one pair at the net, and the other at the baseline. The pair on the baseline have the option of trying to pass their opponents, or of trying to lob them. If the lob (3) is successful, the pair at the net retreat, and the pair at the baseline can come into an advantageous position at the net.

TEAMWORK
Doubles is all about teamwork. Ken Flach and Robert Seguso are one of the best doubles pairs in the world. Here they are seen in tandem, about to receive a serve. Notice how both players are concentrating hard and watching the opposition. They are in good receiving positions to attack the serve. Note how close Flach is to the center service line, to try to distract the server from hitting down the center line.

 STAR TIP
Have fun and try to win from the net, but always work together as a team.

ACTION STUDY (1): SERVE AND VOLLEY

If you possess a good serve and enjoy volleying, you may well find that the tactic of serving and volleying is for you. It is particularly suitable for fast surfaces (such as grass) where the ball rebound is quicker, and the ball can be put away more easily. You will find that a lot of top players, particularly men, serve and volley when they play at Wimbledon. Boris Becker has won Wimbledon with some devastating serving and volleying. Martina Navratilova has also had great success using this tactic. The type of player who uses serving and volleying tries to get to the net whenever possible. A position near to the net has both psychological and physical advantages.

One of the keys to good serving and volleying is being able to vary your serve by changing the spin — flat, slice or topspin — and by varying the direction or placement in the service box. This means your opponent doesn't know what to expect, and cannot get into a rhythm on his returns. You need to follow your serve into the net as quickly as possible, forcing your opponent to rush his return. Try to steady yourself so that you are balanced before hitting the volley

SPLIT STEP
The split step is the key to making your serve and volley work, even at beginner level. When coming into the net, you need to stop momentarily as the receiver strikes the ball, in order to be balanced and react to the return. You jump slightly off one foot, and land on two feet. This gives you a base from which you can move either to the forehand or backhand side to play your volley.

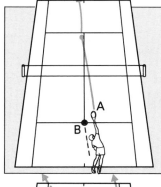

THE RIGHT POSITION
It is very important that you get into the right position for your first volley. If you serve down the center line (A) you will run in down the center of the court (B). This serve will reduce the angle of return from your opponent, and is very useful in doubles.

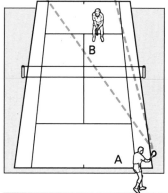

MIDDLE OF ANGLE
If you serve out wide, you must follow the path of the ball, and you will move slightly to the side of the center line (A) to cover possible angles of return. A wide serve will open the court up for an easy volley into the open space, but it will also give your opponent (B) a wide range of angles with which to pass you.

IN ACTION
Pat Cash won the men's title at Wimbledon in 1987 with some magnificent serving and volleying. He was very quick to follow his serve into the net. Here he is stretching for a backhand volley off a good return of serve.

INSET: Pat Cash serving.

 STAR TIP
Learn from top players and try practicing serving and volleying.

ACTION STUDY (2): BASELINE PLAY

1 Many people play tennis from the back of the court and rarely venture to the net, particularly on a slower surface, where it is difficult to put the ball away because the opponent has more time to chase it. As ground strokes are bread-and-butter shots, you will probably learn to play from the baseline before serving and volleying. A good baseliner such as Chris Evert has solid ground strokes and will be very consistent, making few unforced errors. In a match, more points are lost than won. If you can be consistent from the back of the court, you will have a lot of success.

2 A good baseliner will hit the ball about 2-3ft (60-90cm) above the net – this gives a good margin for error. Mistakes are often made at beginner level with the ball landing in the net. Give yourself a bit more height, and play the percentage shot (i.e. the easier one). If you hit higher over the net, it will help you to get good length, then your opponent will find it difficult to do much with the ball, and with luck you will force him into making an error. Try to hit the ball over the net into zones A and B. Zone C should only be used for aggressive passing shots.

3 Clay-court tennis can be like a game of chess, and the rallies tend to go on for a long period of time. A simple tactic often used by top players is to force their opponent from one corner to the other. The aim is to run the opponent from corner to corner, until you force him out of position. In the diagram, player A hits a forehand cross-court to the sideline, and then hits the return cross-court to the backhand. Player B is running from side to side, and eventually hits a short return to point C. Player A then has three chances to win the point: he can hit cross-court to point 1; wrong-foot his opponent if he is running hard to cover the shot, by hitting to point 2; or slice the ball short and wide, to point 3.

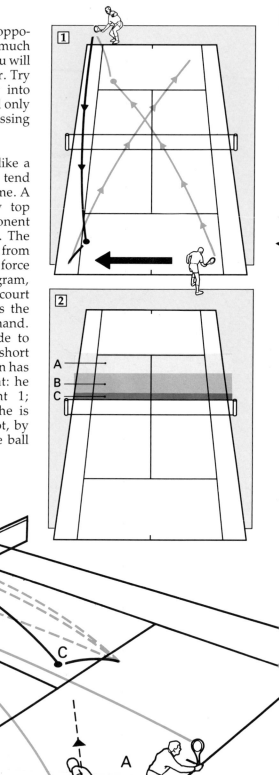

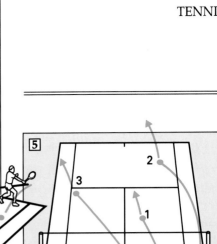

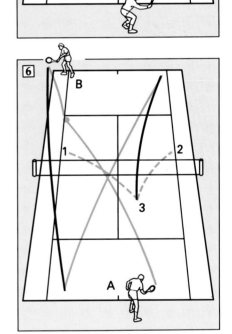

FORCING SHOTS
ON BACKHAND

4 Another tactic which you will see top players like Ivan Lendl using is a sequence of forcing shots from the backhand side. On a slow court, the rallies will go on for several shots. The diagram simply shows a few strokes to finish the point (otherwise it would be too confusing to read). Player A hits deep backhands to player B, driving him further to the left each time. Both players are trying to recover to the central position on court after each shot. Eventually, player B hits a short ball to point C.

This opens up the court for player A to hit a deep backhand 1 down the line, if player B has anticipated this, he could wrong-foot him by hitting a short, angled ball to point 2. This tactic would be used far more by an aggressive baseliner than a defensive one.

5 A good baseliner will not only be able to move his opponent from side to side, but also forward and backward, so that he uses both the length and breadth of the court. Don't forget that sidelines can be used very effectively to take your opponent out of court. One of the best shots to use is a soft topspin shot to the short corner (where the service line meets the sideline). This really makes your opponent move.

Sequence of shots: short ball to 1; lob to 2; then short, angled ball to 3.

6 You must vary your shots — use different spins (topspin, flat or slice) — and vary the pace of the ball so that your opponent cannot get into a rhythm. One way to vary your baseline game is by the use of the drop shot, which if played at the correct time can be an outright winner or at the worst open the court up for an easy next shot.

Player A hits wide to player B's forehand, taking him well out of court. Player B retrieves the ball and hits it down the line. Player A then hits a deep cross-court backhand, forcing a short ball (3) from B. Player B is still trying to recover to the central position; so player A then fakes another hard drive but as an element of surprise hits a drop shot to 1 or 2. As drop shots can be risky, initially only try them from close to the net. They are probably most effective in the women's game where their court coverage is not so great. Learn from the stars.

ACTION STUDY (3): TO THE NET

Modern tennis has tended to encourage all-court players, who can play from both the baseline and the net. If a ball lands in the middle of the court in a normal rallying situation, during the course of a point, a player has several options: to hit an outright winner, or a short-angled ball, or a drop shot, or perhaps an approach shot.

It is the approach shot that you can try here. An approach shot is any shot which gets you from the back of the court to the front of the court, and into an attacking position at the net. It can be a ground stroke, a slice (particularly effective as the ball stays low on bouncing), or a volley.

An all-court player is always trying to attack the ball, so he will move to any short ball very quickly, hitting an approach shot when appropriate, and coming in to the net. It is easier to hit angled strokes from the net, and it gives your opponent less time to play a return. Remember, though, that it is vital to control the approach shot as you come in to the net.

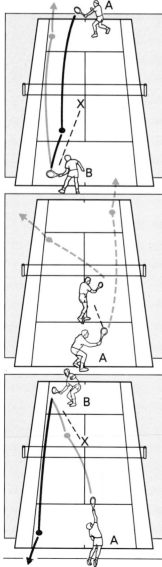

SHORT-BALL RANGE
Each player has his own short-ball range — that is, the ball from which you can get comfortably to the net without being stranded in the middle of the court. When practicing, try to find your short-ball range. Ask your partner (A) to hit balls of varying lengths for you (B) to come in off. Try to get to position X.

DOWN THE LINE: VOLLEY CROSS-COURT
It is important to hit an approach shot deep, forcing your opponent to try to pass you from behind the baseline, and from a defensive position. If you hit cross-court and come in, the court is opened up and it makes it easier for your opponent to hit a passing shot. A simple tactic is for player A to hit down the line, come into the net and volley cross-court.

APPROACH OFF A POOR SECOND SERVE
You can learn when to come to the net by watching top players. You will often see the following: Player A hits a weak serve (generally a second serve) to player B. Player B hits down the line and follows the ball into the net to position X, ready to put the volley away. This is a very effective tactic, but it requires a high level of skill.

ATTACKING THE NET Chris Evert is not renowned for attacking the net, but here she is seen coming in, probably chasing a short ball. The racket head is laid back ready for a sliced approach shot.

 STAR TIP
You must find your own short-ball range to make approaching the net easy.

MENTAL APPROACH

1 Once you have mastered the basic skills of tennis, it is important to become mentally fit or mentally tough if you want to reach a high level of performance. You must think positively. Tennis contains many of the dramas of life – the joy, the pain, the frustration, the uncertainty and the struggle – and you need to be mentally tough to cope with these.

You need to be motivated if you are going to succeed at tennis. The desire to play, train and compete must come from within. All great sportsmen and women are highly self-motivated and possess that inner force which drives them to perform in a certain way. Martina Navratilova possesses tremendous motivation.

2 Your tennis will improve dramatically if you have the ability to concentrate on the task in hand. Learning to concentrate is an acquired skill. A simple way to help yourself is to say "bounce" to yourself every time the ball bounces, and "hit" every time you or your opponent strikes the ball. Tennis is an intermittent game. Small bursts of concentration are required for points, but a longer concentration span is needed for the whole of a match. Monica Seles shows tremendous powers of concentration while waiting to return service.

3 Determination is a vital ingredient in a successful player. Ivan Lendl has sheer will to succeed. He sets himself goals and targets, and works hard to achieve these. On the way to these goals there may well be setbacks, but these will be overcome if you are determined enough.

4 You need to be in control of your emotions – for instance, when you get bad line calls or when playing conditions are bad. Mats Wilander is obviously upset here, but he hasn't resorted to racket throwing. If you are getting annoyed, a good routine to follow is to take a deep breath, and breathe out slowly.

5 Chris Evert is perhaps the best example of a player staying calm and relaxed during a match. She has been nicknamed the Ice Maiden for this reason. You will play better tennis when you are not experiencing nervous tension. Due to the fact that tennis requires delicate, fine motor skills, it is essential to completely relax and loosen your muscles. Not only must you be physically relaxed, but you must also feel calm inside.

6 Some players, particularly those with a creative mind, use a simple technique of visualization to perform better. This simply involves using your imagination to think without using words, creating pictures in your mind. Messages are then sent to the brain. These closely resemble the messages sent to the brain during physical action. Gabriela Sabatini is sitting in the chair at the change of ends with her eyes closed. She might be using this technique. Close your eyes and think of your favorite player, remembering how they play a particular shot. Imagine you are playing the same shot, and then go out and try to be that player on court. It is fun to do this, and it can give good results.

7 A true champion is very self-confident and Jimmy Connors is no exception. You need to believe in yourself, in your own ability, and believe that you are equal to the task. It is vital that you have a realistic attitude towards performance, and acknowledge the fact that you will sometimes perform badly. Don't forget that confidence is specific, and that nobody is confident in all situations all the time. Confidence often comes from successful experiences, so if you are a beginner at tennis remember: the more times you hit the ball over the net, the more confident you will feel playing that shot.

8 A player is always fully responsible for his own actions and John McEnroe is no exception. Your destiny is always in your own hands, so if you blow a fuse in a match and slam balls around you get a warning or a penalty point from the umpire. Remember, it was your responsibility.

9 Tennis is fun and you must always try to enjoy playing. If you enjoy playing you will perform, but as soon as tennis ceases to be fun performance problems inevitably arise. Invariably you will play well if you *have fun*. This feeling of enjoyment and fun will help you to stay calm, relaxed and optimistic. The struggle, the battle, and the confrontation can all be fun. A truly great competitor, like Michael Chang, loves the struggle of competition as well as the feeling of success.

10 Whether you win or lose, tennis is only a game. You must learn to accept defeat gracefully, without getting angry. Bad losers whine, complain and make excuses. They never say they have lost a match — it was too windy, they didn't feel well, their opponent was lucky, there was a bad line call, and so it goes on. Try to acknowledge the fact that perhaps you were beaten by somebody better than yourself. Conversely, if you win, don't be too arrogant or disrespectful to your opponent. Feel happy, but remember your opponent might well feel dejected and disappointed. Boris Becker acknowledges the fact that he has played a great match with Henri Leconte here. It takes two people to do this.

SCORING

The scoring system used in tennis is often very confusing for a beginner, because it does not follow a logical pattern. The system in use today originated from Real Tennis, in which 15, 30 and 40 were all minute points on a scoring clock.

At the start of a game both players have a score of "love" (0-0). The server's score is always called out first. If the server wins the first point, the score is fifteen-love (15-0) (one point to the server and no points to the receiver). If the receiver then wins the next point, the score becomes fifteen all (15-15). If the score reaches forty points each (40-40), then the score is called "deuce." A player has to win two points in a row from deuce to win the game. If the server wins the first point from deuce, the score is "advantage server." If the server then wins the next point, it is "game to the server"; however, if he loses the next point, the score returns to deuce.

At the end of the first game, the players change ends. They do so after every odd-numbered game; 1, 3, 5, etc. If the score at the end of a set is 6-4, the players change ends after the first game of the next set.

A set is won when a player reaches six games, except when the score is 5-5. A player must be two clear games ahead to win, e.g. 7-5, 8-6, etc. Most matches today, however, operate with a tie break system which is used when the score reaches six games all. This prevents very long matches from occurring.

Most tournament matches played are over the best of three sets for both men and women, although in the Grand Slam events (Wimbledon, the U.S. Open, and the French and Australian Opens) men's matches are the best of five sets. This rule does not always hold. In some tournaments, early matches are the best of three sets and later round matches the best of five.

MAIN AIM

The main aim of tennis is to win as many points as possible so that you accumulate more games, and subsequently more sets, than your opponent and win the match. Unfortunately, tennis is a game where many points are lost, but by practicing and learning from top players you can improve your ground strokes, services and volleys. This will hopefully help you to win points, and force your opponent into making errors.

WINNING POINTS

Points can be won by:
1) hitting the ball in such a way that it bounces twice in your opponent's half of the court before he can return it;
2) hitting a shot that your opponent cannot reach 1;
3) serving so well that your opponent cannot return the ball;
4) forcing your opponent into making an error.

It sounds as though it is very simple to win points, but there are even more ways to lose them.

Right: It sounds simple enough – hit a shot that your opponent cannot reach and win a point. Top right: Try and hit the ball by throwing your racket at it and you will lose a point.

LOSING POINTS
Points can be lost by:
1) allowing the ball to bounce more than once before returning it;
2) volleying the ball while standing behind the baseline and making a bad return – if you make a good return, then the rally continues;
3) catching the ball before it has bounced when standing out of court – the ball must bounce before an "out" decision can be made;
4) volleying a ball before it has crossed the net. (The exception is, for example, on a windy day when your opponent plays a dropshot and the wind carries the ball back over the net and onto his half. In this case you are allowed to reach over the net and play the ball, provided you do not touch the net. This is very difficult to do.)
5) throwing your racket at the ball in an attempt to hit it 2 ;

6) touching the net, posts, singles sticks, wood or metal cable, strap, band or ground in your opponent's court while the ball is in play;
7) touching the ball in play, or touching it by anything you wear or carry, except your racket;
8) letting the ball in play hit the ground, a permanent fixture, or another object outside the lines which bound your opponent's court.

Losing points is complex to understand and you might need to consult the rule book. Above all, *learn how to win points.*

TIE BREAK
The tie break was introduced as an alternative to playing advantage sets, and helped to reduce the length of games. In 1969, in the first round at Wimbledon, Pancho Gonzales played Charlie Pasarell in a game that lasted five hours and 12 minutes, with the score 22-24, 1-6, 16-14, 6-3, 11-9 to Gonzales. In fact, the match started on one day and finished on the next!

The tie break comes into operation when the score reaches six games all, and is generally played in all sets except the third or fifth set of a three- or five-set game.

The tie break (and consequently the game and set) is won by the player who first wins seven points, provided he leads by a margin of two points e.g. 7-4, 7-5. If the score reaches six points all, the game is extended until one player is two clear points ahead e.g. 8-6, 9-7.

When the score reaches six games all in a set, the person whose turn it is to serve, serves the first point of the tie break from the right court. Thereafter each person serves two points, alternating between left and right courts, until the tie break is completed. Players change ends after every six points, and at the conclusion of the tie break.

Players often get confused as to whose turn it is to serve after the tie break. Remember that the person who served first in the tie break receives in the first game of the following set.

FITNESS AND TRAINING (1)

The serious tennis player does not increase his fitness playing the game, but trains in order to be "fit to play." The basic components of fitness are speed, stamina, suppleness (or flexibility) and strength. In order to be successful at a high level you also need skill and mental toughness.

•

WITHOUT **SKILL**
YOU CANNOT **PLAY**
•
WITHOUT **FITNESS**
YOU CANNOT **LAST**
•
WITHOUT **MENTAL TOUGHNESS**
YOU CANNOT **WIN**
•

Speed is required to perform movements in the shortest possible time, and in tennis you need speed over a short distance to be able to retrieve the wide balls, the drop shots, the short balls and then to recover, ready for the next shot.

Stamina is the ability to withstand fatigue, but it isn't as important at beginner level when the rallies are not very long! However, as your skill improves, you need stamina to maintain your performance level over a long period, such as three or five sets.

Suppleness is an ability to move parts of the body through a wide range of motions. This is obviously essential in tennis. Every player should warm up and stretch before playing, in the same way that an athlete stretches before training or entering a competition. It is a good habit to get into: it warms you up, reduces the risk of injury, improves your mobility around the court, and can have a useful psychological effect on your opponent. Have a specific routine, where you go from head to toe stretching all the major muscle groups. Try to hold each position for six seconds, but don't bounce.

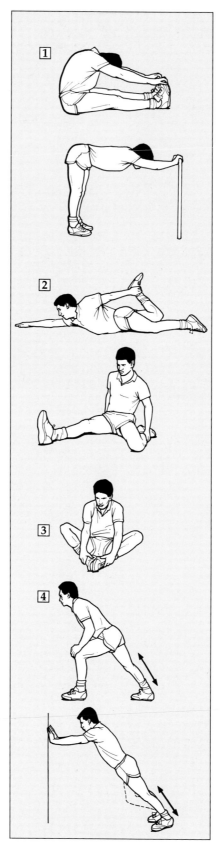

SIMPLE STRETCHING EXERCISES

Try to stretch before playing, and after a big match or a hard training session. Injuries often occur after a match, when your muscles tighten up. Pay particular attention to your hamstrings and lower back, your calves, groin, hips, arm muscles and quadriceps (thighs). Stretching is often used as part of your warm-up; to increase your range of movement significantly, you need a full exercise program.

1 Hamstrings and lower back

2 Quadriceps

3 Groin − sit on haunches with soles of feet facing each other. Press knees down with elbows and hold for at least six seconds

4 Calves − single calf stretch and two-leg calf stretch

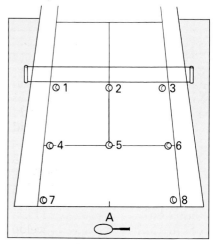

SPEED TRAINING

Speed is needed to get to the ball in time. Three factors are involved: speed of reaction, speed of anticipation and speed of movement. Reaction speed can be improved by performing simple exercises and trying to decrease the time taken. An example is the eight-ball pick-up drill (see diagram above). The player starts from (A) and moves to any of the eight stations. He picks up one ball at a time and returns it to the racket. He repeats this exercise until all eight balls have been collected. The aim is to beat his time on his next attempt.

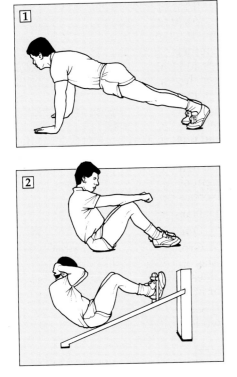

STRENGTH

Strength is the ability to exert force, and a tennis player needs it to get some weight of shot. Strength is particularly needed in the back, legs, stomach, upper arms and shoulders. It is unwise for a young player to do weight training while still growing, although a simple exercise program involving only a player's own body weight shouldn't cause any harm. Press-ups (1) will help to develop strength in the shoulders, and sit-ups (2) will help to strengthen abdominals (stomach muscles).

IT'S A TOUGH GAME

Tennis today is a very tough game and top players have to be very fit. John McEnroe shows his athletic ability in the backhand return of serve, which he has hit while in mid-air. In order to play this shot you need speed of reaction, strength in your legs and flexibility. I don't recommend that you try this shot — yet!

INSET: Pat Cash dives, in an attempt to return a shot.

FITNESS AND TRAINING (2)

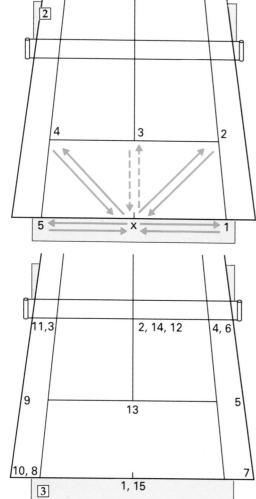

1 SHUTTLE RUNS

In order to improve your fitness and speed around the court, it is a good idea to do some on-court running. One of the simplest exercises for speed is the shuttle run. Drill (A) is for explosive starts and stops to the ball. Sprint from the baseline to the service line and back five times, trying to change direction quickly. Then do the same thing from the baseline to the net. A variation of this is to run forward from the baseline to the service line, and then backward back to the baseline. Try this three times.

In drill (B), the player starts on the outside tramlines and runs to touch each line on the court with his hand, returning to the tramline each time. Try this three times in a row. If you repeat this more times, it becomes a stamina exercise.

2 FAN DRILL

Another very useful speed drill which involves changing direction quickly is the fan drill. Start at position X holding your racket, and run to base 1. Touch the junction between the baseline and sideline with your foot, and the ground in front of you with your racket, and return to the central position X. Repeat this to all the other bases, 2, 3, 4 and 5. Run backwards in both directions to base 3. Repeat this three times, and see how long it takes. On your next training session try to beat this time.

3 TENNIS COURT CIRCUIT DRILL

This drill is another excellent speed drill. It could also be used as a stamina drill, if repeated several times. Follow the route from 1 to 15, running as fast as possible. Run backwards for 4-5, 6-7, 9-10, 12-13. Touch the ground with your hand at each point, and at the front of the court touch the net.

Don't forget to include some stamina work in your training program so that you will be able to maintain your performance levels in long matches.

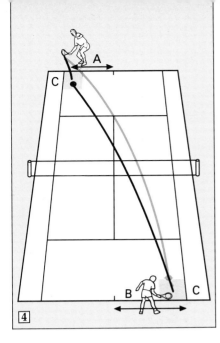

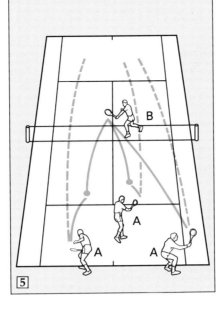

4 CROSS-COURT RALLYING

Many people find that training without hitting a ball is not very stimulating, so I have included some on-court drills here which will improve not only skill level, but also your fitness. In this drill, players A and B are rallying cross-court to specific target areas (C). After each shot they return to the center mark, hitting ground strokes on the run. Try this drill for 4 to 5 minutes; then change sides of the court, and repeat. If you can maintain a rally and really push yourself to return to the center mark after each shot, you will find this is an excellent conditioning drill.

C target
Players move to center mark after each shot

5 GROUND STROKE DRILL

Not only do you need to be quick moving along the baseline, you also need to be able to move quickly to the short ball. Find yourself (A) a practice partner (B) and a large basket of balls. Your partner, armed with the basket of balls, stands near the net and alternates hitting you *short and deep ground strokes*. Your aim is to get to every ball and return if back into court. This will give you a strenuous leg workout. Initially try this drill with 20 balls, and build up to about 50. As a lot of practice involves cooperation between two players, don't forget to change roles and feed to your partner.

6 VOLLEY-SMASH DRILL

The final drill selected is the volley-smash practice. This is excellent for encouraging good movement forward and backward when at the net. It also requires a lot of flexibility, as you will need to really stretch for wide and high balls. Your partner (A) starts with a basket of balls on the baseline and feeds one drive (1) and one lob (2) alternatively, so that you hit one volley (3), and one smash (4).

As soon as you have played the smash, move back quickly to the net, so that you can play the volley. Your target is to make sure that you never let the ball bounce, and that you return every ball into court. Try 25 shots initially, and build up to 40 or 50.

Always try to perform the drills properly – then you will gain most benefit from them. The drills can be performed by beginners and by professionals. The feeding should be easy for the beginner, while the expert would probably be aiming for specific target areas on the court. At the end of your training session, cool down using similar exercises to your warm-up.

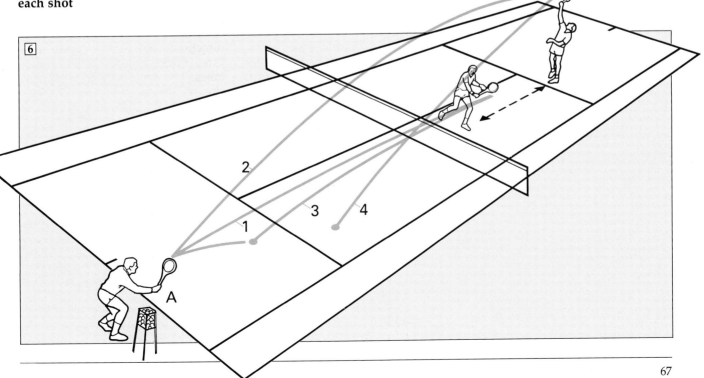

TESTING YOURSELF

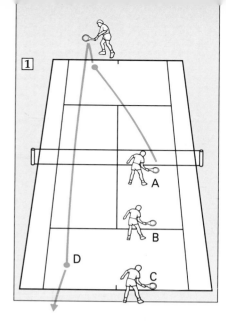

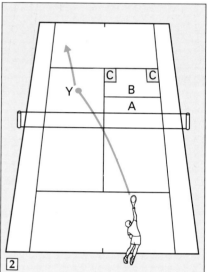

Now that you have learned some of the basics of tennis, it is time to see how good you really are. Try these simple exercises after you have warmed up and stretched. Ideally you will have a practice partner and a basket of at least 20-30 balls. Remember, *planned* practice makes perfect.

1 KEEP A COUNT
Your partner can position himself at the net (A), on the service line (B), or near the baseline (C), while you stand near the baseline on the opposite side of the net. Your partner hits or throws 20 balls to you on the forehand side, and you count how many go over the net and land in the singles court. Repeat this on the backhand side.

Next time, try to beat this score. As your level of skill increases, so the target area decreases – try to hit the ball past the service line and

eventually aim for specific target areas (D) in the back court.

Variation – this could also be done hitting running forehands and backhands. If you start on the center mark, run wide and hit the ball down the line.

Once you have become confident with your ground strokes, particularly the forehand, move on to the serve, so that you can play a game.

2 SERVING DRILLS
The serve is the one stroke over which you have complete control – you toss the ball up and you hit it. It is also the one shot you can readily practice by yourself. The initial aim is to serve the ball over the net into the box (Y), diagonally opposite. Try 20 serves to the right court, and 20 to the left. Count how many serves are "good" and land in the correct area. Again, as your level of skill increases, mark out areas in the service box and aim for these. Score as in the diagram.
**Area A – 1 point Area B – 2 points
Areas C – 4 points**

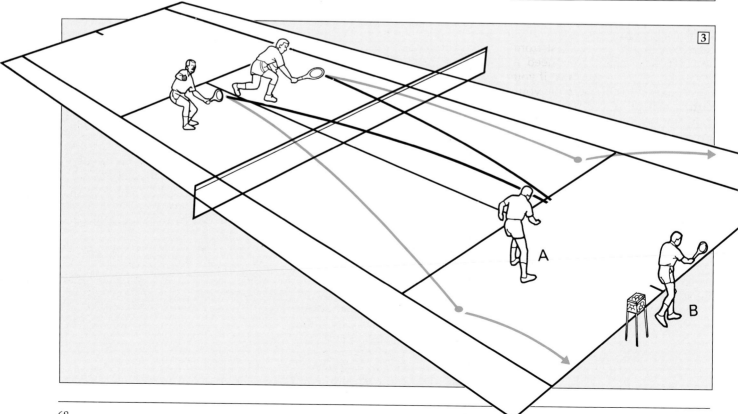

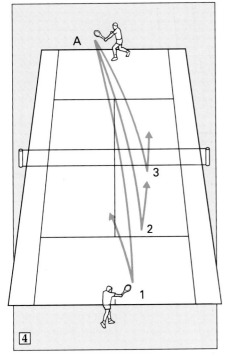

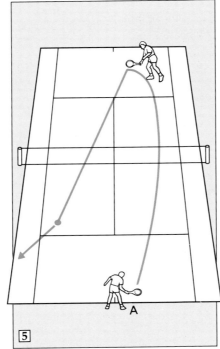

[3] VOLLEY TEST

Now try a simple volley test from near the net. Again, you need a partner and a basket of balls. If you are a beginner, it is best for your partner to hand-feed balls to you at shoulder height from the service line (position A). Try 10 volleys on the forehand side and then 10 volleys on the backhand side. Count how many go into the singles court, but don't knock your partner over in the process! If you have an accomplished partner, he could hit balls by racket from the baseline (position B) for you to repeat this exercise. If you find this too easy, try to hit every volley past the service line, or to even smaller target areas.

[4] GROUND STROKES AND VOLLEYS

This exercise will really test your skills, as you now have to link the shots from the back of the court with those at the front. Your partner stands near the baseline (A), and hits one deep ball (to position 1), one mid-court ball (to position 2) and one short ball (to position 3) so you in turn hit a ground stroke from the baseline, an approach shot from the middle of the court and finally a volley from the front of the court. You score one point for each ball which lands in the singles court. Try 10 sequences, and record your score out of 30. To increase the level of difficulty, try to hit each ball past the service line.

[5] SMASH

Another shot that you need to practice from close to the net is the smash. This test will depend largely on the ability of your partner, and whether or not he can feed a reasonable lob to you.

Your partner (A) stands just behind the baseline with a basket of balls, and hits 20 lobs to you. Try to smash every ball back into court.

How many can you make out of 20 attempts? To make it more difficult, smash past the service line or to a specific target. If you are really feeling energetic, run in and touch the net after each smash — this encourages you to get back into a good net position after each smash.

[6] RETURN OF SERVICE

The final test is for your return of service — the second most important shot in the game. Your partner (A) serves 10 balls from the right court in to area X, and then 10 balls from the left court, into area Y. As returner (B), your main aim is to get the ball back over the net and into court. Count how many returns you make. Once you can get the ball over the net, aim past the service line.

Have fun as you try these exercises. As your level of skill improves, try for specific target areas (C).

GLOSSARY

Approach shots − forcing shots which enable a player to attack the net.

Australian formation − used to describe the positioning of players in doubles when the server's partner stands on the same side of the court as the server.

Back-court − area from the service line to the baseline

Backhand − stroke played with the playing arm across the body, and the back of the hand facing forward.

Backspin − ball hit with spin so that it rotates backwards.

Backswing − initial swing of the racket to prepare for forward stroking motion.

Baseline − back line at either end of the court.

Baseline game − method of play used by players who stay on or near the baseline and rarely come to the net.

Baseliner − person who plays from the back of the court (the baseline).

Block − type of action used on the volley. There is little takeback and little follow-through.

Center mark − mark on the middle of the baseline used to bisect the court.

Center service line − line that divides the two service courts in half.

Checkstep − move from one foot to land on two prior to contacting the ball − very evident when serving and volleying.

Chopper grip (Continental grip) − specific way of holding the racket, normally used for volleys and the service.

Clay court − type of court surface on which the ball rebound is slow. (See also slow court.)

Closed racket face − head of racket is tilted downwards, with strings facing down slightly. Used when hitting with topspin.

Contact point − the point where the ball meets the racket strings.

Cool-down − to slowly bring the body to rest after exercise (also known as warming down).

Court − playing area for tennis.

Cross-court − stroke that drives the ball diagonally across the court.

Defensive lob − shot which is generally hit very high in the air, to allow a player to recover his court position.

Defensive smash − smash normally hit from a deep lob. Can be hit for a winner, but is generally used just to keep the rally going.

Deuce − even score after six points.

Double-handed backhand − backhand hit with two hands, close together on the racket handle.

Doubles − a game of tennis with four players, two on each side of the net.

Down the line − parallel and close to the sideline.

Drill − method of training by repetition of exercises.

Drive − ball which is hit after the bounce.

Drive volley − volley normally played from mid-court, often hit with topspin.

Drop shot − ground stroke hit with a lot of backspin, so that the ball bounces very close to the net.

Drop volley − volley hit with backspin so that it just drops over the net.

Eastern backhand grip − grip used to hit a backhand drive. Found by turning the hand a quarter of a turn inward from the Eastern forehand.

Eastern forehand grip − grip used to hit a forehand drive. The palm of the hand is behind the handle.

Falling ball − a ball coming down from the top of its bounce.

Fast surface − surface on which the ball will rebound quickly, e.g. grass.

Fitness − the capacity of a player to perform. A general term to encompass strength, speed, stamina and suppleness.

Flat serve − a hard-hit serve without topspin.

Flexibility − ability to move parts of the body through a wide range of movements.

Floating return − a return without a lot of pace.

Follow-through − path of racket after hitting the ball.

Forehand − stroke played with palm of hand facing the front.

Front court − area between the service line and net.

Game − the unit of scoring when a player has won four points, or has won two consecutive points from deuce.

Grand slam − name given to the four major tournaments: the French Open, Wimbledon, the U.S. Open and the Australian Open Championships.

Grip − method of holding the racket. Also covering of the racket handle.

Ground stroke − stroke used to hit the ball after it has bounced. Collective name for forehand and backhand drives.

Half-volley − stroke hit just after the ball has left the ground.

High volley − volley played well above shoulder height.

Left court (advantage court) − name given to the left side of the court.

Lift − term used to describe the path of the ball on the backhand (when the ball is hit to a high level to get it over the net).

Lob − ball which is hit high into the air.

Lob volley − volley hit high over opponent's head when at the net.

Low volley − volley played when the ball comes low over the net, forcing the player to bend down.

Match − predetermined number of sets which will decide a winner. Women play the best of three sets; men play either the best of three sets, or the best of five sets.

Mental toughness − to have control of your inner self.

Mid-court − the area around the service line.

Net play − refers to all shots played near the net.

Offensive lob − ball hit upwards, *just* out of the reach of an opponent, generally with topspin.

Offensive smash − overhead shot, generally hit from close to the net for a winner.

Open racket face − head of racket slightly tilted upward, with the strings facing upward.

Open stance − player positioned facing the net, often used when hitting topspin drives.

Overhead − another name for a smash. Shot hit with the racket above the head.

Passing shot − a stroke that drives the ball past an opponent who will usually be at, or approaching, the net.

Percentage shot − hitting the shot which is most likely to give you success.

Permanent fixtures − include net, posts, single sticks, cord or metal cable, strap and band, back and side stops, stands, fixed or moveable seats and chairs around the court and their

occupants, all other fixtures around and above the court; also the Umpire, Net Court Judge, Foot-Fault Judge, linesman and ball boys when in their respective places.

Place up (toss) − method of putting the ball into the air on the serve.

Point of impact − point at which the racket meets the ball.

Punch − racket action used on the volley.

Rallying − series of ground strokes.

Ready position − place from which a player starts, prior to contacting or moving to the ball.

Receiver − the player who receives serve.

Return of service − shot used to return the service.

Right court (deuce court) − name given to the right side of the court (normally referring to the service box).

Semi-western grip − grip used to hit a forehand drive.

Serve volley − simple

method of play. The server follows the serve into the net, to play a volley.

Server − the player who puts the ball into play.

Service − the act of putting the ball into play.

Service box − area into which the server aims the ball.

Set − unit of scoring whereby a player has won six games, but must win by a margin of two games, e.g. 7/5, 8/6, or in the case of a tie-break 7/6.

Short ball − ball that lands close to the net, or midway up the court.

Short-ball range − ball from which a player can comfortably get to the net, without being stranded in the middle of the court.

Short tennis − scaled-down version of tennis, played on a badminton-size court, generally with plastic rackets and foam balls (indoors), and a low net.

Shuttle run − moving backwards and forwards between two places.

GLOSSARY

Sidelines – lines at either side of the court which mark the boundaries of the playing area.

Singles – game played one against one.

Singles sticks – posts used to support the net when singles are played on a doubles court with a doubles net. Posts are positioned 3ft (0.91m) outside the singles court on each side.

Slice – stroke hit with side-spin.

Slow court – surface on which the ball rebound is slow – suitable for baseline play. (See also clay court.)

Smash (overhead) – shot hit with the racket above the head.

Speed – ability to cover a distance in the shortest possible time.

Spin – rotation of ball in flight.

Split-step – term used for jumping off one foot and onto two, to get balanced.

Stamina – ability to withstand fatigue.

Stance – position of a player when about to strike the ball.

Strength – ability to exert force.

Suppleness – ability to move parts of the body through a wide range of movements.

Swing – path of the racket on ground strokes.

Tactics – methods used to implement a game plan.

Takeback – method of moving the racket back from the body on various strokes.

Technique – method of playing a stroke.

Tramline – the space between the singles sideline and the doubles sideline.

Throat of racket – shaft of racket, the part between the head of the racket and the handle.

Throwing action – path of the racket on the service and smash.

Tie-break – system of scoring that can be used when the score reaches six games all, as an alternative to the advantage set.

Topspin – forward rotation of the ball.

Toss (place up) – method of putting the ball in the air to begin the serve.

Two-handed backhand – backhand drive, with two hands on the racket handle.

Visualization – process of creating pictures or images in your mind.

Volley – name given to the stroke played before the ball bounces.

Warm-up – method of preparing the body before vigorous activity.

Western forehand grip – method of holding the racket with the palm of the hand underneath the handle.

INDEX

A

Agassi, André 14-15
all-court player 58
approach shots 46, 58-9
Australian Open 21, 62

B

backhand 12-15, 18-21
  grips 12-15, 45
  one-handed (single)
    18-19
  slice 46-7
  smash 36
  topspin 44-5
  two-handed
    (double) 13-15, 20-21
balls, tennis 9
baseline tactics 56-7
baseliner 56-7
Becker, Boris 22-3, 36-7,
  48-9, 54, 61
blocking action 28-31
Borg, Bjorn 45

C

calf muscle 64
Cash, Pat 54-5, 64-5
Chang, Michael 44-5, 61
chopper grip 22, 28
clay courts 9, 45, 49, 56
clothing, tennis 8-9
concentration 60
Connors, Jimmy 13, 14,
  26-7, 34-5, 50-1, 61
continental grip 10, 22,
  28, 49, 50
cool down 67
court 6-7

D

determination 60
doubles 6, 52-3
  positions 52
drills 66-9
  cross-court rallying 66
  fan drill 66
  ground stroke drill 66
  tennis court circuit drill
    66
  volley-smash 67
drop shot 40-1, 57, 58
  backhand 40-41
  forehand 40-41

E

eastern backhand grip 12,
  45
eastern forehand grip 10
Edberg, Stefan 12, 30-1
emotions 60
Evert, Chris 13, 56, 58-9,
  60
exercises, test yourself
  68-9

F

fast surfaces 54
Fernandez, Mary-Joe 21
fitness 64-7
Flach, Ken 52-3
flexibility 64
forehand 10-11, 16-17
  drive 16-17
  grip 10-11
  topspin 42-3
French Open 62

G

Garrison, Zina 46-7
Gonzales, Pancho 63
Graf, Steffi 4-5
Grand Slam 62
grass courts 9, 54
grip, size 8
groin muscle 64
ground strokes
  drills 66, 68
  spins 42-7

H

half-volley 32
hamstring muscle 64

L

Leconte, Henri 61
Lendl, Ivan 10-11, 57, 60
lob 38-9, 52
  backhand 38-9
  forehand 38-9
losing points 62-3

M

McEnroe, John 61, 64-5
Mayotte, Tim 32-3
mental approach 60-1
motivation 60

N

Navratilova, Martina 16,
  50, 54, 60

O

open stance 10, 17

P

Pasarell, Charlie 63
passing shot 42
Pernfors, Mikael 42-3
positioning on court 16
punch action 28-31

Q

quadriceps muscle 64

R

rackets 8-9
  junior 8
  weight 8
ready position
  ground strokes 16, 18
  serve 22-5
  volley 28, 31
relaxed condition 60
return of service 26-7, 69
running 66

S

Sabatini, Gabriela 8, 42-3,
  61
Sanchez, Arantxa 9
scoring 62-3
Seguso, Robert 52-3
Seles, Monica 13, 20, 60
self-confidence 61
semi-open stance 17
semi-western grip 10, 17
serve and volley
  doubles 52
  singles tactics 54-5
service 22-5, 48-51, 54
  drills 68-9
  flat 49
  grip 22
  second 50, 58
  slice 50-1
  stance 22-5
  topspin 48-9
shoes, tennis 9
short tennis 6

T

short-ball range 58
shuttle runs 66
singles 6
slice
  ground strokes 46-7
  serve 50-1
slow courts 45, 49
smash 36-7, 67, 69
speed 64, 66
  training 64, 66
spin 42-51
  on ground strokes 42-7
  on serve 48-51
  slice backhand 46-7
  topspin 42-5
split step 54
stamina 64, 66
strength 64-5

T

tie break 63
topspin
  backhand 44-5
  forehand 42-3
  serve 48-9
training 64-7
two-handed backhand
  grips 12-15
  stroke 20-1

U

U.S. Open 4-5, 62

V

visualization 61
volley 28-35, 67, 69
  backhand 30-1
  drills 68
  drive 35
  drop 35
  forehand 28-9
  half 32
  high 32
  lob 35
  low 32-3

W

warm up 64
western grip 10, 17
Wilander, Mats 14, 28-9,
  60
Wimbledon 9, 31, 54, 62-3
winning points 62